LEOŠ JANÁČEK

na památku p. Dr Han-
Hollandrovi !
Brno 11. června 1928

LEOŠ JANÁČEK

His life and work

HANS HOLLANDER

Translated by Paul Hamburger

ST MARTIN'S PRESS
NEW YORK

FIRST PUBLISHED IN GREAT BRITAIN 1963
BY JOHN CALDER (PUBLISHERS) LIMITED
17 SACKVILLE STREET - LONDON, W.I
ALL RIGHTS RESERVED
COPYRIGHT © HANS HOLLANDER 1963

FIRST PUBLISHED IN THE U.S.A. 1963
BY ST MARTIN'S PRESS INC.

175 FIFTH AVENUE

NEW YORK 10, N.Y.

LIBRARY OF CONGRESS CATALOG CARD NO: 63-11071

MADE AND PRINTED IN THE REPUBLIC OF IRELAND BY
HELY THOM LTD., DUBLIN

CONTENTS

CONTENTS (*continued*)

APPENDICES

ILLUSTRATIONS

PREFACE

THIS BOOK was written with the intention of providing the music lover of the Western world with a contemporary study of Janáček's life and work. It was hoped that the book could be published on the thirtieth anniversary of Janáček's death (1958), but for technical reasons publication has been delayed until the present date.

Since Janáček's death, interest in his work and his unique personality has increased so rapidly and become so widespread, that the need for a factual account of his life's work and an introduction to his spiritual world can no longer be ignored. Because his work consists for the greater part of vocal music—folk song settings, choruses, cantatas, operas, the *Glagolitic Mass*—the position Janáček has secured in the international scene of modern music has been primarily that of an operatic composer. In this process of international recognition, the national and regional aspects of his art have been appreciated as highly attractive and individual, despite the fact that they serve in some way to limit the universal significance of his work.

In this book an attempt is made to show the full range of Janáček's artistic achievement, and in particular the importance of his instrumental and chamber music; furthermore, I have tried to elucidate the philosophical, the ethical and the personal vision that gave rise, not only to his operas and choral works, but to all his compositions.

As is the case with many great musicians—and indeed many creative artists in general—Janáček's gifts were not confined to a genius for music alone. One could justly call him a philosopher and, in the spiritual sense, a teacher, a seeker of truth. He was also a great psychologist endowed with an unusual insight into the mysteries of the human soul; he was a great fighter, a man with a big loving heart, altogether a personality of stature. These characteristics lent his style its specific quality and imbued it with an ethical and eternal-humane truth from which ultimately, the timeless impact of his music springs.

Whether Janáček tends towards realism, verismo or impressionism, is of secondary importance. What makes his music so singularly fascinating is the inner strength and depths of his vision; the micro- and macrocosmic relevance of his musical message so characteristically fused with the folkloristic impulse of his inspiration; his understanding of and concern for the ultimate issues in life, and the compassionate glow in his music when it expresses the agony of human suffering. It is not easy to dissociate Janáček's art from these extra-musical concerns. It might be said that these social, ethical and philosophical conceptions, so closely linked with psychology, mark Janáček's *oeuvre* as a characteristic manifestation of the early Twentieth Century. Moreover, he anticipates contemporary trends by the development of his style from short melodic fragments into form-units of spacious architectonic design. His method of thinking in terms of condensed and minute musical entities is very modern, and—notwithstanding his occasional leanings towards impressionism and expressionism—his technique of melodic and rhythmic variation and transformation is alive with possibilities that point to the future. This way in which Janáček realises the latent possibilities of development, both musically and psychologically, is one of the secrets of his originality. His capacity for transcending the popular raw material of his music and raising it to the sphere of the all-humane, is a measure of his greatness.

Leoš Janáček has often been described as a 'naturalist', an unbridled *enfant terrible*, contemptuous of tradition, established technique and disciplined craftsmanship. That his art answers to its own profound inner laws, that Janáček never wholly renounced a certain classical-romantic traditionalism which again came to the fore in his last creative period, is something I hope to prove conclusively in this study.

Janáček's position in Czech national music, and in particular his relationship to Smetana and Dvořák, is another problem to which I have given some attention. There is no doubt that together with Smetana and Dvořák, the Moravian Master can be counted among the great representatives of the Czech musical genius in recent times. These three composers form a trinity of special talents, characteristic tendencies and clearly defined individualities; the nationalistic element in their work supplies the common denominator. Though their artistic personalities are clearly defined, their mutual position in Czech musical history appears as a complementary and at the same time inevitable phenomenon. The urban Czech patriotism of Smetana with its cosmopolitan overtones is in contrast to the naïve, earthbound pan-slavonic nationalism of Dvořák, and is developed and complemented by the dynamic social-humanitarian Slavism of Janáček with its Eastern orientation. These three great Masters of Czech national music represent three vital sectors in the national history and psychology of the Czech people; their influence permeated the whole of Czech music and cannot be overestimated.

During the last years of his life, I enjoyed the privilege of a close association with Janáček, and thus had the opportunity of coming to know many of the Master's thoughts and artistic projects. In a professional capacity, I knew some of Janáček's pupils—B. Bakala, P. Haas, Dr. L. Kundera, V. Petrželka, and others—as well as the noted Janáček biographers and specialists, Professor Vladimír Helfert, Professor Jan Racek, Dr. Karel Vetterl, Dr. Bohumir Štědroň and Professor Adolf E. Vašek. These people—some of whom are no longer living—have supplied me with important, and largely unknown information. I wish to record my sincere gratitude to them. A special word of thanks is due to my friend Dr. Karel Vetterl for his unstinting advice, particularly on folkloristic matters, and to Professor Jan Racek for the readiness with which he placed at my disposal the most recent findings in Janáček research. For various valuable suggestions I am indebted to Dr. Mosco Carner, and Messrs Martin Cooper, Edward Lockspeiser and Donald Mitchell, and particularly to Miss Pamela Lyon for her most helpful advice concerning the presentation of the text. Lastly I should like to acknowledge the assistance given me by music publishers and editors of books and periodicals who have kindly given permission for the reproduction of quotations, music examples and photographs. My thanks are due to:

> Artia, Prague, for permission to reproduce pictures and quotations from B. Štědroň's book *Janáček—Letters and Reminiscences*.
>
> Augener Ltd., London, for permission to use music examples from Moussorgsky's *Pictures at an Exhibition*.
>
> Czechoslovak News Agency for permission to reproduce a picture.
>
> Les Editions Rieder, Paris, for permission to reproduce a picture from Daniel Muller's book *Janáček*.
>
> Hudební Matice Umělecké Besedy, Prague, for permission to quote music examples from Janáček's *Taras Bulba*, *The Fiddler's Child*, the *First* and *Second String Quartets*, 26

Popular Ballads, Maryčka Magdonová, Folk Poetry of Hukvaldy in Songs.

Matice moravská, Brno, for permission to quote from Jan Racek's study *Slovenské prvky v tvorbě Leoše Janáčka.*

Pazdírkovo nakladalství, Brno, for permission to quote from Vlad Helfert's book *Leoš Janáček* and for the use of pictures from that book, also for permission to use music examples from *On an Overgrown Path.*

Philharmonischer Verlag, Wien, for permission to use music examples from Janáček's *Sinfonietta.*

G. Schirmer, Inc., New York, for permission to quote music examples from *The Musical Quarterly*, vol. XLI, No. 2.

Státní nakladatelství krásné literatury, hudby a umění, Prague, for permission to use music examples from the *Diary of a Young Man Who Vanished*, and to quote from the *Musikologie*, vol. 3.

Universal Edition, Wien, for permission to use music examples from Janáček's *Jenufa, Kátà Kabanová, The Cunning Little Vixen, The House of the Dead*, and the *Glagolitic Mass*, and to quote from Max Brod's book *Leoš Janáček.*

H.H.
1963

I

JANÁČEK'S LIFE

CHAPTER 1

JANÁČEK'S ANCESTORS

CHILDHOOD IN HUKVALDY

THE FIRST of Leoš Janáček's ancestors to emerge from the obscurity of the past and meet us as a historically authenticated personality was a Kašpar Janáček who in the year 1697 settled in Frýdek in North Eastern Moravia. During the eventful age of the counter-reformation, this busy small town was already important as a cloth-weaving centre. It may have been the better earning prospects held out by this place that prompted Kašpar Janáček to leave his rural village, Smilovic near Těšín (Teschen), and to move to town, where he soon found employment as a weaver. For a hundred years, his descendants followed the weaving trade in Frýdek. As is shown by the sparse documents we have, they were honest artisans without higher spiritual or artistic aspirations. Music seems to have played no part at all in the lives of these ancestors of the great Moravian composer.

Not until the end of the Eighteenth Century do we find a more clearly defined personality among the composer's ancestors. This was Jiří (George) Janáček (1778-1848), the grandfather of Leoš Janáček; with him the social and intellectual advance begins that culminates in the creator of *Jenufa*. Jiří's widowed mother had in 1784 entered the service of a Father Ant. Herman of Velký Petrvald (Gross Peterswald) in Silesia as a housekeeper. Herman who, besides his pastoral duties, concerned himself with the development of the village-school, seems to have devoted himself to the education of the fatherless boy At the early age of nineteen, we find Jiří as assistant schoolmaster in Velký Petrvald; an office which in those days included such diverse duties as wood-chopping, cleaning the school house, supervising the schoolmaster's children, running errands, ringing the church bells—but also playing the organ. In the biographical notes of his son Vincenc[1], Jiří is described as a man of energetic, even violent temperament; he was a good organist and organ-builder and an able improvisator on his instrument; he was also a singer, wood-carver, bookbinder and schoolteacher. Nothing is reported of any gift for composition. Four of his sons inherited his mental faculties, two becoming priests and two reputable schoolteachers.

Despite his many-sided abilities, Jiří Janáček's career did not take him further than a schoolmaster's post in the Silesian village of Albrechtice, where he died on October 15th, 1848. If Jiří introduced the realistic and musical element in Janáček's ancestral line, his wife Anna, née Scheutter (or Šajtar, 1783–1869) strengthened the peasant root of this hardy stock. Bound to a restless husband who later took to drink, it was she who lent the marriage the necessary stability and domestic order. Thus, the famous grandson's basic traits of personality appear prefigured in the characters and dispositions of his grandparents.

On the 4th of October, 1815, Leoš Janáček's father, Jiří the younger, was born as the fifth child of his parents. His life, which was spent in the narrow confines of the Moravian-Silesian border-country, was not devoid of interesting moments and richly human experiences. His career was predetermined by that of his father. He too became a school teacher and organist; however, he was destined to continue the paternal tradition and talent on a higher, more cultured plane. His early musical upbringing took place in

[1] *The life of Jiří Janáček* ("Životopis Jiřího Janáčka") was written by his son Vincenc in 1897. Like his father, Vincenc was a schoolmaster. Besides the above mentioned biography, he also wrote a chronicle of the parish of Albrechtice.

Velký Petrvald where he was given tuition in piano and organ-playing and in singing by the local choir-master, Josef Richter. At the age of sixteen, we find him as a school assistant in Neplachovice near Opava (Troppau, 1831), a place which, owing to an encounter of momentous consequences, is of extraordinary significance in the biography of the younger Jiří. Here, the boy Pavel Křížkovský (1820–85) was given to him as a pupil, the same Křížkovský who subsequently, as a composer and founder of modern Czech choral music, and above all as a teacher, was to exert a decisive influence on Leoš Janáček. Vincenc Janáček tells of this in the biography of his father: 'There (in Neplachovice) he (Jiří) was sought out by a little orphaned boy, Pavel Křížkovský, whose mother asked him (Jiří) to teach the boy music and singing. He accepted him as a pupil, and by preparing him to gain a scholarship at the Convent of the Holy Ghost in Opava he laid the foundation of his subsequent position as a composer. The composer Křížkovský later on in Brno repaid Leoš Janáček all the kindness he had received from his father Jiří.'

A year he spent as assistant teacher in Kateřinky (Katherinental) near Opava (1833–34) brought Jiří valuable practical experience with regard to the church music of the Silesian capital. His next post as assistant teacher, later as schoolmaster, at Příbor (Freiberg) in Silesia (1834–48) deepened and matured his abilities as a teacher and organist. Thanks to the presence of the Piarist order, Příbor was able to look back on a tradition of church music that was far above the average. This tradition was to a certain extent still alive during the first half of the nineteenth century; and as it happened, the music at the deanery church had once more taken a turn for the better at about the time of Janáček's engagement.

On the 24th of July 1838, Jiří Janáček married Amalia Grulichová, the nineteen-year-old daughter of a Příbor publican. She brought a dowry of 200 florins into the marriage; and, of equal practical importance, her burgher origin conferred certain social advantages on her husband which, in turn, permitted them some prosperity and personal comfort.

Příbor too, however, was to be only a stepping stone in the career of this aspiring man. In the revolutionary year of 1848, the post of headmaster in Hukvaldy fell vacant, and in September of that year, the Janáček family moved into this little mountain village near the Silesian-Polish border. The appointment of Jiří Janáček as schoolteacher and choirmaster in Hukvaldy lasted to the end of his life (1866). They were years of exhausting struggles, full of privations and painful disappointments. School affairs were in a bad state here and had to be entirely reorganised by the energetic teacher. The village was poor, comprising in all eighty-three registered dwelling houses with one hundred and thirty-seven habitations. Many school-age children stayed away from lessons because they lacked clothing. Some linen weaving was done in the place, and sheep were bred as far as the poor ground allowed; but these were hardly sufficient to support the six hundred inhabitants. Besides, Hukvaldy had until 1848 been a feudal domain belonging to the archbishopric of Olomouc (Olmütz), and therefore continuously exposed to the pressure of the manifold restrictions and burdens of such a situation. The personal and official circumstances of the schoolmaster were not rosy. His yearly salary amounted to two hundred florins, a sum which, in view of his steadily increasing family, was far from sufficient. Furthermore, the schoolhouse was in bad repair, the heating arrangements unsatisfactory, and the dampness of the rooms proved highly injurious to good health. In repeated petitions to the episcopal authorities, alternatingly humble and energetic, did Jiří Janáček seek to improve his domestic situation, but it was not until he lodged a personal protest with Archbishop Fuerstenberg that he achieved a belated, and only partial, alleviation of matters (1858).

In such distressing circumstances was Leoš Eugen Janáček born on the 3rd of July 1854, as the tenth child of his parents. Amalia Janáček had presented her husband with fourteen children in all, but only nine had survived the first years of their life. Despite all economic difficulties, this household was not lacking a certain idyllic charm. Organ-playing and domestic music-making, the cultivation of forty-eight beehives and an orchard—it is the image of a bucolic existence such as corresponded to the ideals of the age of enlightenment and the post-Rousseau century. On the other hand, the upheavals of the revolutionary period around 1848 had not passed by the family of the Hukvaldy teacher. The national emancipation of the Czech people was in the air, and the attending hopes and expectations had taken a strong hold on the minds of Czech patriots. In his writings, Vincenc Janáček regrets that Jiří the elder should not have lived to see the great events of the revolution: '... then came the year 1848, when the sun of freedom shone on all the peoples of Austria. Oh, how he was interested in all those great happenings, but he was visibly declining and we realised that his days were numbered.' It is certain that the introduction of Czech as the teaching language in Hukvaldy must have deeply satisfied the patriotic Janáček. Determined and progressive in the practise of his profession, he enlarged the curriculum of the school on his own initiative, and introduced drawing, geography and singing as compulsory subjects. In his official testimonial he is described as a 'very able teacher' and 'very industrious'.

But outside his school too, Jiří Janáček served the cultural life of Hukvaldy well. One year before his death (1865) he founded, in accord with the prevailing national awakening, a singing and reading circle in Hukvaldy. This circle soon developed an amazing activity. We know of several concerts in which choruses, usually of national tendencies (Škroup, Tovačovský, Slavík, etc.), were performed; the repertoire is said to have included also a mass of Josef Haydn. The conductor of the choir was Jiří

Janáček's eldest son Karel (born 1844).

Notwithstanding this increase in his activities, the days of Jiří Janáček were numbered. His many privations and the effects of his unhealthy living quarters brought on serious attacks of gout and a heart disease to which the high-minded man fell victim on the 8th of March, 1866 in his fifty-first year. After his death, the personality of Amalia, the composer's mother, comes more to the fore. This resourceful and courageous woman now took up life's struggle on behalf of herself and her numerous family. Her roundish, thick-set figure and lively, pleasant features are the physical heritage that she handed on to her famous son. Through her inborn practical musicality she also contributed to the artistic inheritance of Leoš Janáček. She is said to have had a pleasant soprano voice; more uncommon, however, was her talent for organ playing; and a significant light is shed upon this capable woman by the fact that until the re-appointment of the Hukvaldy organist's post was effected, she exercised the office of her late husband herself for six months to the fullest satisfaction and approval of the authorities.

The question has often been discussed whether and to what extent the Hukvaldy milieu influenced the artistic development of Leoš Janáček. In the memoirs he wrote at the end of his life[1], the composer has not much to say about these early years in his parents' home. The poverty in his family, and in general the hard struggle which the inhabitants of that infertile land of forests and hills had to put up, left distinct marks on Janáček's personality. We hear nothing of early impressions of a fanciful, aesthetic or romantic kind, nothing of that vague playfulness or dreaminess which usually characterises the talented child of comfortable circumstances. From the start, Janáček's upbringing was directed to practical matters. First place was taken by music, as is tradi-

[1]Autobiographical sketch, published by Adolph Veselý: *Leoš Janáček, Pohled do života a díla*. Prague, 1924.

tional in a family of schoolmasters and organists. In the neighbouring village of Rychaltice there was a larger church than in
Hukvaldy, and they often needed extra singers or instrumentalists.
Then the father would walk over with two or three of his
children to help them out. 'I with my pleasant discant;' Leoš
Janáček reports in his memoirs, 'my sister with her viola; the
choir was full of singers and players on these occasions. There
were a lot of desks, and the gold-painted organ with its many
stops at both sides of the manuals, and at the back by the window
two enormous kettledrums.' In such a realistic way did the boy
Janáček see his surroundings. Again and again we meet him at
the church choir of Hukvaldy or Rychaltice, as a singer and,
sometimes, surely as a kettledrum-player, for this instrument
fascinated him most of all. He was still too young to take a very
active part in the endeavours of the choral society. But the
ardently patriotic ambition of these singers and of the compositions performed by them did not escape this alert boy. Here are
the roots of his future choral works with their rugged rustic and
social pathos. At the village school, he was an indifferent pupil—
it seems that he was affected by the worries which the steadily
declining health of his father caused the family. Thus, the
reminiscences of his early years are totally lacking in any gaiety
and child-like carefreeness. As Vladimír Helfert says, it seems as if
here, already, Janáček's significant tragic A flat minor was
sounding forth from the depth of his youthful experiences.

CHAPTER 2

APPRENTICESHIP

THE ST. AUGUSTIN ABBEY OF BRNO

At the age of eleven, in September 1865, Leoš Janáček entered the St. Augustin Abbey in Old Brno as a boarder. He was an 'exhibitioner', that is, he was in the possession of a scholarship that covered both his living expenses and the musical education he received at the monastery.

He was meant to finish the last year of his primary school education in Brno while at the Abbey (1865-66). This decision may have been taken by his father in order to lighten the expenses of the Hukvaldy household, while at the same time using his son's vocal talent to advantage. In furtherance of his school education, Janáček in the years 1866-69 took the three-year course of the Old Brno Junior Secondary School, and from 1869 to 1872 he studied for his teaching degree at the State Teacher's Training College in Brno. Not music, but a teaching career, traditional in his family, was to be the goal of Janáček's vocational studies.

The venerable abbey of Old Brno had originally been a Cistercian foundation of the Fourteenth Century. Its late-gothic church with the baroque chapter house are today overshadowed by the growing city and the industries that are concentrated in the district of Old Brno. In Janáček's days, the St. Augustin Abbey had reached one of the peaks in its long history. Father

Pavel Křížkovský (1820-85) had in 1848 been entrusted with the direction of the church music, and under the influence of this sensitive musician and efficient organiser, the abbey had gained a leading role in the musical life of the Moravian capital. Many well-known names—musicians, learned men, politicians—are closely associated with the St. Augustin Abbey. Heinrich Wilhelm Ernst (1814-65), for instance, the violin virtuoso and subsequent pupil of Paganini, who was born at Brno, received his first musical education here. Later on, the Augustinian pater Gregor Mendl (1822-84) conducted the famous botanical experiments connected with his theory of genetics in the abbey garden.

It may have been the previous acquaintance of Janáček's father with Pavel Křížkovský that smoothed the way for granting the scholarship to Leoš. Křížkovský knew full well, however, that in the young schoolmaster's son from Hukvaldy he had acquired for his chorus a musical singer with a good alto voice. To be sure, the priest-musician and Czech patriot could not then have foreseen that the four years which Janáček was to spend at the abbey would prove to be of fundamental importance for his development.

Meanwhile, however, things took a turn for the worse for the boy transferred to this unfamiliar world of town and abbey school. Janáček's father had died in March 1866, and this event signified a tragic demarcation line in Leoš Janáček's life. As he put it in his Memoirs: 'My world, my very own world was to begin now. It was to embrace everything. My father dead—the cruelty of it is unimaginable.' In these words of self awareness one feels the nascent realisation of his own strength. The parental home ceased to exist for Janáček. His mother left Hukvaldy soon after her husband's death, and it is strange how little we know about her influence on Janáček's education during those years. On the other hand two new figures enter the youth's life: Father Pavel Křížkovský and the curate Jan Janáček, one of his father's brothers.

Křížkovský must undoubtedly be credited with having decisively influenced the intellectual and musical education of the young Janáček. But he was also a good friend to his pupil. He looked after the modest contributions sent by Janáček's uncle, often eking them out by adding from his own funds when important purchases had to be made, and he intervened with the school authorities when Janáček's progress was unsatisfactory. The strict discipline which Křížkovský imposed on the Old Brno church choir (Janáček had the position of leading alto in it), his own artistic integrity, his Czech patriotism which is reflected in his stirring male choruses, all these laid the foundation for the personal and artistic culture of his young pupil. In accord with the contemporary trend of Cecilianism[1] Křížkovský concentrated on vocal and polyphonic works in the church-music of the Old Brno Abbey. The repertory included works by Lassus and Vittoria besides contemporary Czech and German works, and in the study and performance of all these works, Janáček took an active part, first as a singer, later as a choral conductor. It is obvious that this special training greatly enhanced his sensitivity towards the style and technique of vocal writing. Apart from his singing, Janáček's piano playing and the knowledge of elementary theory he had acquired in Hukvaldy, were developed and intensified by Křížkovský.

But the young Janáček's patriotic ambitions, too, owe their historical and philosophical foundation to the atmosphere of the Old Brno Abbey; one could even say that under the influence of the national-religious movement centred around the figures of St. Cyril and St. Method, which was being very actively supported by the St. Augustin Abbey, Janáček's nationalism was diverted into its specific Moravian and Eastern-Slavonic channels.

[1]The Cecilian movement originated in Germany during the second half of the Nineteenth Century. Its chief aim was the restoration of liturgical purity and dignity in roman-catholic church music in the face of the increasing worldliness of the late-baroque orchestral masses. Accordingly, the Cecilian movement stood for a revival of plainchant and the Sixteenth Century vocal polyphony as represented by Palestrina and his school.

In the year 1863, the millennium of the arrival of the two Slavonic missionary saints on the soil of the Great-Moravian realm was celebrated. Six years later (1869), the millennium of St. Cyril's death was commemorated with great ecclesiastical, and at the same time political, demonstrations in Moravia. The two national saints, Cyril and Method, were not only the symbols of Christianity's triumph over the heathen aborigines of Moravia, but even more, they were seen as the legendary representatives of the greatness and might of the former Great Moravian realm. But it was not only the memory of a long-past kingdom on Moravian soil that was connected with the two saints. Did the thought of their missionary work not bring in its train the awareness of the proud pan-Slavonic past springing from common cultural and literary roots, with its unified alphabet created by Cyril; and was all this not fuel for the idea of a great national future? A national movement steadily gaining momentum had been born on Moravian soil, and Leoš Janáček was seized by its fever.

The national pride which Janáček had inherited from his forebears, received a powerful fillip from the Cyril-Method cult. In 1869, he took part, as a boy-singer, in the jubilee celebrations at the abbey-church in Velehrad, the legendary seat of the first bishop of Moravia, St. Method. Though he had little interest in the liturgical splendour of the proceedings in the mighty baroque church of Velehrad, or, for that matter, in this catholic demonstration as such, he was strongly stimulated by the sight of the thronging participants in their colourful, richly decorated traditional costumes and by the broadly flowing exuberance of their church singing. In this manifestation of the peasants and common people from the provincial towns of Moravia and near-by Slovakia he felt the inherent autochthonous element, the revelation of an earth-bound strength. There was a strong social element in the national ambition here, for as members of a national minority in the old Austrian state these people were in many respects subject to economic as well as political pressure, and had been relegated to a socially inferior position. All this struck deep roots in the soul of young Janáček, and the reverberations of his experience remained a source of inspiration for the rest of his life.

From this period of patriotic enthusiasm we have a letter of the fifteen-year-old boy to his uncle, the curate Jan Janáček, with the urgent request to buy him a national costume; a piece of 'Russian linen' was needed for it, and a tailor could surely be found in the Old Brno Abbey who would make the suit at a reasonable price. 'Russian linen'—for the first time Leoš Janáček directs his eye to the Slavonic East. With this suit he means to show his Slav sentiments, his racial and national individuality in a homeland that had been unlawfully usurped by the German 'intruders'.

Next to Pavel Křížkovský, the uncle Jan Janáček played an important role in the young man's life. Jan Janáček was curate of a small village in the neighbourhood of Bystrice, a place of pilgrimage in Moravia, and subsequently curate of the village of Znorovy. Numerous letters from Janáček to him are a proof of the fatherly care and affection he felt towards the ageing man, who in other respects, too, appears as the benefactor of the family. While Křížkovský supervised the spiritual and musical education of Janáček, his uncle must surely have exerted the best possible influence on the human and moral development of the youth. The question arises here as to the effects this predominantly male influence during Janáček's decisive years of development—his mother steps further into the background—had on the psychology of the mature man and artist. His subsequent philosophy of compassion and his intensive eroticism may well be traced back to those harsh early years in which he was surrounded by a purely paternal atmosphere, lacking the warmth and mellowing counterbalance of maternal love. His remarks about his mother in the year of his father's death (1866) are of a strange melancholy in which the presentiment of a deep forlornness and anxiety about the future seem to mingle. 'In the square of the abbey, my mother leaves me with a heavy heart. I am in tears, so is she. Strange, heartless people. A strange school, a hard bed, even harder bread. No more caresses.' Like a gloomy nightmare is the description of the stay in a Brno lodging-house before Janáček's entry in the Abbey (September 1865); probably the last night spent by the eleven-year-old boy under the care of his mother. 'In fear, my mother and I spent the night in one of those dark chambers—it was on the Capuchin Square. I did not sleep a wink. At the first grey of day—out of the house, into the open.'

But in spite of his loneliness and emotional constraint, the years spent by Janáček in the Old Brno Abbey were essentially a positive phase of his life. The curriculum aimed at practical, everyday music making, containing, as it did, daily singing, piano, chamber music and orchestral rehearsals as well as thorough-bass exercises. This gave Janáček an invaluable basis of craftsmanship which in future years was repeatedly to secure for him his technical superiority over fellow-students. In his wind-sextet *Mládí* (*Youth*), written in the evening of his life, he has set a loving, serenely contemplative monument to his years in the Old Brno Abbey.

The following years at the Brno Teachers' Training College[1] offered Janáček an opportunity for making good some omissions that were due to his one-sided schooling at the Old Brno Abbey. In the first place, he had to fill many gaps in his general education, and it is significant that his best results during the final examinations were in Czech language and History. Here, a new vista opens into the future: the artist Janáček who subsequently was to use his mother-tongue in a most original and personal manner, who was to base his musical inspiration on the niceties and

[1]From 1872 to 1874, Janáček did the prescribed probationary period as teaching candidate at the 'Imperial and Royal Slavonic Teachers' Training College' in Brno.

peculiarities of this language, is already recognisable in his essays and oratorical exercises. The centre of his interests, however, was music. Janáček, who until now had lived almost exclusively in the spiritual world of church music, passionately grasped the opportunity of becoming conversant with secular music, and particularly with that of his day. Beside the classics, it was chiefly German late-romanticism (Wagner, Liszt) and the increasingly important national Czech music which excited his interest.[1] In addition, he played the organ at the Old Brno Abbey and frequently conducted its choir, as well as other choirs of the town, as for instance the Beseda Brňenská and the choral society 'Svatopluk'. In the main, however, he worked at his further theoretical schooling, and in this endeavour he soon reached the point where a lack of stimulus, resources, and above all, of artistic personalities in the provincial milieu forced new decisions on him.

During his probationary period as Teaching Candidate, Janáček was also active as piano teacher, probably in order to make a modest living. We know that in those days he had a happy, unclouded love affair with one of his pupils, the sixteen-year-old Ludmila Rudišová, the daughter of a Brno factory owner. She remained the star of his heart for the next two years, until a very much stronger tie gave a new direction to his emotional life. It was his friendship with Zdenka Schulz, the daughter of Janáček's immediate superior, the director of the Teachers' Training College, Emilian Schulz. This understanding and benevolent pedagogue deserves a special place in the early biography of Leoš Janáček. Apart from Křížkovský, it was he who fully recognised the outstanding musical gift of the young man, and not only encouraged him in his decision to choose music for a career, but also gave him his active support. Through Schulz' help, Janáček succeeded in obtaining a place at the Prague

[1]Smetana's *Bartered Bride* was first performed in Prague in 1866; his *Dalibor* in 1868.

Organ School, and it was due to the initiative of this good man that the young musician was able to spend some valuable time abroad, in Leipzig and Vienna.

Being an experienced church-musician and a pupil of Křížkovský, it was natural for Janáček to continue his training along the lines he had hitherto pursued. Schulz as well as Křížkovský recommended the Prague Organ School directed by F. Z. Skuherský. In order to understand this peculiar choice, apparently so remote from Janáček's real vocation, one must remember that in the opinion of all concerned, Janáček's career seemed to tend in the direction of choral conducting and organ playing. He was considered the rightful successor to Křížkovský, particularly on the strength of his modern leanings which stamped him as the predestined modern reformer of Czech church music begun by Křížkovský. Janáček, to be sure, was to fulfil these expectations in his own way when, at the end of his life, he composed the *Glagolitic Mass* on an old Slavonic liturgical text.

CHAPTER 3

WANDERINGS

IN THE EIGHTEEN-SEVENTIES the Prague Organ School under the direction of F. Z. Skuherský (1830-92) enjoyed the reputation of being the best, and at the same time the most progressive educational institute for church music on Czech ground. Skuherský himself was an energetic, occasionally despotic character; a musician of great practical and pedagogical experience— he was the author of two books on composition—and moreover of decidedly modern orientation. The ideas of contemporary music, still very controversial in those days, and particularly the melodic-harmonic innovations of the Wagner circle (chromaticism, enharmonic modulation) were given a place in his curriculum side by side with the training in strict polyphonic style and in the use of ecclesiastical modes. Furthermore, Skuherský's teaching supported the reform of church music under the aegis of Cecilianism that was also advocated by Křížkovský.

In these circumstances, it was certainly logical that Janáček at twenty should decide in September 1874 to continue his training at the Prague Organ School. By reason of his previous schooling, he was given permission to skip the first of the three years that made up the full course of studies; he began at once with the curriculum of the second year, simultaneously crowding the topics of the third year into his working schedule. This

Janáček's birthplace, the School House at Hukvaldy

St. Augustin Abbey at Brno

The composer's mother

Pavel Krížkovský

Antonín Dvořák

Janáček in the National Čamara

concentration of all his energies towards accomplishing a given task, under high if self-imposed pressure, is as characteristic of Janáček the man and the artist as the unforeseen and brusque manner in which his Prague episode was to conclude.

Here already, at his first step into the world, a basic dynamic law of Janáček's life manifests itself. His actions are often marked by restlessness and impetuosity; by an urge for fully absorbing a situation spiritually and emotionally, and with an intensity that does not allow for any deliberation or reflection. This spontaneity, changeability and explosiveness is deeply stamped in the rhythm of his life, and his strongest works of art evince the enduring signs of this elemental dynamism.

The financial basis of Janáček's Prague sojourn has not so far been clarified. So much is certain that he lived in very straitened circumstances, occupying a small, dark, unheated room next to the porter's lodge, and suffering hunger most of the time. A Brno friend, by name of Neumann, to whom he had handed on some of his piano-lessons, loyally sent to him the full fee of five florins in monthly remittances. Moreover, he found a friend's help in Prague, too: Father Ferdinand Lehner, the publisher of the periodical *Cecilie*, which was in sympathy with the current reform of church music, not only obtained a pianoforte for the impecunious young man, but also prevailed upon him to contribute to his magazine. In it, Janáček frequently published short reviews about musical events in the capital, and it was this activity that was to bring a sudden end to his studies at the Organ School. The occasion was a choral concert under Skuherský which Janáček criticised adversely for being insufficiently rehearsed. Skuherský was not the man to pocket such an affront. Janáček had been his best pupil; moreover, Skuherský had felt personal affection and sympathy for the highly gifted young man. Perhaps his reaction was the more violent for this reason. Janáček had to leave the Organ School immediately (March 1875)—a decision, however, which was soon taken back, once the director had calmed down again. All the same, Janáček's stay in Prague had drawn to an end. The Organ School had given him all it could, and the next phase of his training clearly shows in what direction his future career was to develop. Janáček left Prague in July 1875.

Let us now consider what he gained from his studies in Prague. The principal subject had been composition, under the guidance of Skuherský. Harmony, simple and double counterpoint, imitation and fugue; and besides, organ playing, thorough-bass and improvisation—these subjects which are the equivalent of a curriculum of nearly three years were mastered by this student of genius within eight or nine months. In addition, he pursued aesthetic studies, read much, and endeavoured to give a clear direction and secure basis to his spiritual and artistic outlook. His exercise books from those days are extant, and they provide interesting information about the earliest phases of his musical thinking. In his harmony exercises, for instance, it becomes apparent that he was nothing less than enthralled by the chromatic-enharmonic style of his age. Yet at the same time, Janáček's personal manner already comes to the fore in various details, as, for instance, when he abruptly curtails a modulatory progression and plunges headlong into the new key—a practise, incidentally, to which Skuherský took no exception. Furthermore, the sing-able, lyrically conceived melodic line so characteristic of Janáček's mature art, can already be found here.

Janáček's melodic-harmonic thinking was in those years decidedly late-romantic. All the more interesting, therefore, is the fact that his aesthetic notions about form and content of a work of music and about classicism and romanticism moved in a dramatically opposite direction. From the aesthetic writings of Zimmermann[1] and Durdík[2] he took the ideas of an abstract

[1] Robert Zimmermann, *Allgemeine Aesthetik als Formwissenschaft*, 1865.
[2] Josef Durdík, *Všeobecná aesthetica* (General aesthetics), 1875.

formalism which tallies in essentials with Hanslick's formal-aesthetical dogma.[1] Classical formalism and objectivism, giving ideal and well-proportioned expression to the beautiful, are accepted by Janáček as the supreme aesthetic principle. In consequence, he rejects the subjective and romantic, and above all, the unbridled, unstylised and naturalistic—even opera and music drama. We see that in the process of developing he had to fight his way through phases which eventually were to prove quite foreign to his true artistic personality. This is not unusual. At bottom, Janáček's has never been a theorising or aestheticising mind. But his acquaintance with Hanslick's form-idealism gave to his feeling for style and form an enhanced assurance, which, together with his technical studies under Skuherský, represented a further major progress in his development. Even in his later years, he repeatedly gave expression to his high regard and gratitude for Skuherský's tuition.

Prague had given to Janáček's mental horizon the extensiveness he needed so that he might absorb cultural values conducive to maturity. During his stay at Prague, he must surely have come to know one or another contemporary Czech work. Dvořák's star was rising, and it is certain that Janáček's strong affinity with this artist was just then receiving its first impulses. At that time, Janáček entered into personal relationship with Dvořák—a relationship that was to become one of the happiest and most valuable of his life. We also know that on the occasion of a concert conducted by Smetana, the young Janáček was deeply affected by the master's deafness which was noticeable to all. Even at that time, Janáček was conversant with the Russian language and the Russian alphabet, for he used the cyrillic script for intimate entries referring to his love for Ludmila Rudišová, which are scattered through his exercise books. He also worked hard at his French, and, of course, at his German.   -

[1]cp. Eduard Hanslick, *Vom Musikalisch Schoenen*, 1st edition, Leipzig, 1854.

Janáček's studies at the Prague Organ School concluded with a final examination which he passed with distinction, and during which he played on the organ a chorale-fantasia of his own composition on the Toccata and Fugue in C major by J. S. Bach. But somehow, the twenty-one year old Janáček was still not set on the right course. First of all, he sought to acquire a secure basis for making a livelihood by obtaining a state degree as music teacher. In 1876, he gained this degree, thereby establishing the musical character of his career as a state-certified teacher.[1] As such he remained active at the Brno Slavonic Teachers' Training College until the summer of 1879. He also visited Prague, and it is likely that he perfected his knowledge of form and orchestration under Skuherský's guidance. All these activities, however, are only a transition, a gathering together of strength for his proper vocation.

Janáček's friends in Brno, particularly the far-seeing Emilian Schulz, felt he was destined to be a creative musician and that it was necessary for him, therefore, to enrich his artistic taste and perfect his technical training. Janáček himself felt a desire to see the world, and above all, to hear a lot of music. For some time he thought of continuing his studies with Anton Rubinstein at St. Petersburg (Leningrad). He had heard Rubinstein in Prague, and subsequently in Leipzig, and the latter's rigorous, inspired manner of interpretation, and the romantic colourfulness of his compositions had made a deep impression on Janáček. But Schulz' advice was to study in Germany, and thus, having obtained (again with Schulz' help) the necessary leave from the Austrian school authorities, Janáček decided to enter the Royal Conservatoire of Music at Leipzig in September, 1879.

This institute, with its high reputation dating back to the days of Mendelssohn and Schumann, and its essentially classical and

---

[1]According to his original training, he should have become a teacher of Czech language and literature, with music as a secondary subject.

conservative tradition, seemed the right place for Janáček in view
of his prevailing artistic orientation. Here again, he plunged
himself into his work, and there were days when his overwrought
nerves brought him to the brink of a collapse. Composition was
again his main subject. He acquired the routine of writing in all
forms; polyphony and fugue, in particular, were for several
weeks his special hobby-horses. By October, he had written no
less than twenty exercise fugues. This enormous labour, however,
helped him in realising what his proper career was to be. At the
time of his arrival in Leipzig, Janáček had still toyed with the
idea of a virtuoso career; he hesitated between the piano and the
organ. But he soon discarded this plan and came down on the
side of composing. '. . . I know all about concert-giving and its
consequences, and I am convinced that it does little toward
immortality and fame. My goal lies not in this direction.[1]' He
now concentrated on the study of the musical forms and, also,
practised the organ and the piano, the latter, however, only in so
far as it could be useful to him as a composer. Among the teachers
of the Leipzig Conservatoire who made a strong impact on
Janáček were Dr. Oscar Paul (Harmony, Counterpoint, Pianoforte, Aesthetics, History of Music), Leo Grill (Musical Form,
Pianoforte), Ferdinand Wenzel (Pianoforte) and Wilhelm Rust
(Organ)—not so, however, Carl Reinecke (Choral Singing).
Janáček's impulsive temperament gave preference now to one,
now to another teacher; in general, however, Grill's solid method
of instruction seemed to suit him best.

Janáček was very lonely in Leipzig. The unfamiliar atmosphere
of the German town, the many new artistic impressions, the
pressure of his self-imposed working schedule, his growing doubts
in the competence of certain teachers, and not least his separation
from Zdenka Schulz—out of all these tensions there arose a grave
crisis which was only to subside somewhat when, with the agree-

[1]From a letter of Janáček to Zdenka Schulz, October 18th, 1879.

ment of his Brno friends, Janáček decided to leave Leipzig.
Nevertheless, Leipzig was for him one of the most important
experiences of his apprenticeship. What hitherto he had been
missing, namely an acquaintance with the great works of classical
and romantic music, had now been supplied. He attended the
concerts at the *Gewandhaus*, the performances of sacred music at
the St. Thomas Church, and frequent chamber music recitals.
He now entered the world of Beethoven, particularly of his last
period (C sharp minor Quartet, late sonatas), of Schubert's C
major Symphony, of Schumann's Symphonies, of numerous
cantatas by J. S. Bach, and many other works. He was deeply
moved by Beethoven (though subsequently he was strangely to
modify his view of him); Brahms left him cold; he sought to
familiarise himself with French music, though Leipzig offered
scant opportunity for this; however, he worked through
Berlioz' treatise on instrumentation, and at one point he thought
of continuing his studies with Saint-Saëns in Paris. All this
widened his artistic horizon enormously. There was no opera in
Leipzig, but in any case, it was the problems of instrumental
music Janáček was grappling with during this period of his
classical-formal instruction. A whole series of compositions came
into being, amongst them his op. 1, Variations for Piano on an
original theme (composed between January 29th and February
22nd, 1880)—'They are quite nice,' he wrote to Zdenka Schulz,
'and I consider them my first entirely correct work'—furthermore, Three Romances for Violin and Piano, a Minuet for Piano
('Zdenka's Minuet'), and many other things— ... 'ideas fly
towards me like birds.'

Janáček spent only the winter months from October 1879 to
the end of February 1880 in Leipzig. He soon found that here,
too, the possibilities of further advancement were exhausted, and
so by Easter 1880, we find him back in Brno, full of new plans,
and above all, inspired with his love for Zdenka Schulz.

The relation of Leoš Janáček to Zdenka Schulz, his future wife, was one of the strangest, and at the same time most rewarding human experiences of his life. At first sight, the differences between the two young people seem so great that one should scarcely have thought them capable of entering a lasting union. Zdenka Schulz (born 1865, died 1938) came from a patrician family of German sympathies and strictly conservative middle-class principles. Her mother's family were Prussian-Silesian petty nobles; her father was the son of a physician from the district of the North Bohemian town of Mělník. His career was typical for an Austrian secondary-school teacher who, living in a bilingual district, was equally at home in the Czech and German languages and stood, therefore, in official bilingual employment. In Zdenka's parental home, German only was spoken, except with the servants, and she herself did not acquire a knowledge of Czech until later life.

Janáček had first met Emilian Schulz in 1872, when the latter took over the directorship of the Slavonic Teachers' Training College in Brno. Soon, the young teaching candidate gained the confidence of his superior who not only strengthened his resolution to take up an exclusively musical career, but also put piano lessons and conducting jobs in his way. Thus, in 1877, Zdenka too became Janáček's piano pupil. '. . . I was very much afraid of my teacher,' she writes in her memoirs. 'I knew him slightly from the institute and had heard from his pupils that he was very strict . . . He was slim, of small stature, his pale face forming a startling contrast to his hard, brush-like full beard, his heavy black locks and his very expressive brown eyes. Even then I had come to like his small, full, white hands which turned into animate, independent beings as soon as they neared a key-board . . .' This is how this well-protected girl, living in a dream-world, as it were, saw the future partner of her life. There was something shy and romantic in her attitude to the rugged, at first

glance so wild and mysterious-looking man of the people. Did
Zdenka have a presentiment that it would be her mission in
Janáček's life to soothe, clarify, stabilise—and, if truth be told,
to endure much? It is certain that Janáček had opened to the
impressionable girl a richer and fuller world than that in which
she had habitually moved. On the other hand, her uncommon
intelligence and sensitivity enabled her to understand Janáček's
ideas, to strengthen his self-respect, and frequently to give a
practical turn to his plans. For Janáček, who, as we know, cannot
be said to have experienced the educational rewards of a secure
home, the affectionate family life in Zdenka's home must have
been a great blessing. Here, he acquired social polish and personal
sureness of behaviour that is developed by intercourse with
understanding friends in an atmosphere of comfort. The Schulz
family-circle became Janáček's second home; he was understood,
given advice, and granted every support.

His love letters to Zdenka from those days count among the
most beautiful confessions of this kind we have from any artist.
Often they are soliloquies, self-analyses; then again stormy
outbreaks of passion; there is wooing in them, and a certain fear
of losing the precious treasure, which gave meaning to his life
and inspiration to his work. It is strange to think that the recipient
of all these outpourings was a fifteen-year old girl, and one
involuntarily asks oneself whether Janáček was not investing
Zdenka in his mind with more maturity than she naturally
possessed at the time. Yet Zdenka must have been an extraordinary girl—she calls Clara Wieck to mind, who at the same
tender age had through her love and rare understanding given
inspiration to the aspiring genius of Robert Schumann. External
conditions, however, were much more favourable in the case of
Janáček's courtship than they had been in that of Schumann, and
as early as 1881, Janáček was able to marry his young bride.

Janáček's choice of German cultural institutes for his further studies was most likely due to the influence of the Schulz family; likewise, his holiday journey to Germany in the year 1878 had been prepared by these friends. On that occasion, he visited the Bavarian town of Öttingen where there was the firm of Steinmayer which had recently delivered a new organ to the Old Brno Abbey. On this journey, he also saw Munich and Berlin. In the relaxed holiday mood of those weeks, Janáček composed his string suite *Idylla*.

But let us return to the eventful years of 1879-80. With another six months of official leave at his disposal, Janáček resolved to enter the Vienna Conservatoire for the summer term of 1880. He was accepted as a second-year student of composition (teacher: Franz Krenn) and pianoforte (teacher: Josef Dachs), and arrived in the Austrian capital on April 1st, 1880. In the musical life of Vienna, which at the time was divided into two rival camps, the Conservatoire of Music and Dramatic Art of the Philharmonic Society under the direction of Josef Hellmesberger was on the side of the progressive party of Wagnerians, represented by Anton Bruckner and Hans Richter. Janáček, the formalist of classical-conservative tendencies stood, as it were, in the opposite camp, that of Brahms and Hanslick. Right from the beginning, he was doubtful whether the teaching method followed by Krenn was in agreement with his own strict principles. He criticised the 'Wagnerian bombast' in the efforts of his colleagues, stressing, by way of contrast, the 'solidity' prevalent in Grill's class at Leipzig. 'I myself must now be my strictest teacher,' he writes to Brno, 'for I cannot reckon here with revisions as strict as those practised by Grill.' In Vienna, once more the law of his impulsive restless-ness is obeyed—with even greater force now, owing to the increasing independence and self-reliance of his own artistic personality. His creative powers are mounting. Within a very brief space of time, he composes a violin sonata, a cycle *Songs of Spring* (on very indifferent texts by Zusner) and a string quartet.

All these works are lost now; they were probably destroyed later on by Janáček himself.

In Vienna his crisis was swiftly approaching its climax. At the end-of-term prize-giving for students' work, the slow movement of his Violin Sonata was rejected as being too academic. He was deeply hurt by this. Convinced as he was of the artistic value and technical solidity of his work, he felt unable to accept the decision of the reading panel, which he considered unjust. At the end of May he gave notice of his decision to discontinue his studies; he did not even wait for a testimonial.

This was the end of Janáček's studies. He was now twenty-five years of age but he was one of those creative musicians who mature slowly—fate had granted him a generous life-span—and we find that young Janáček, at an age when others had already written the masterpieces of their life was still trying to find himself, still ignorant of his own idiom and artistic aims. On the other hand, his technical mastery was complete. He had perfect command of harmony and counterpoint, was conversant with all forms, handling them with a well-nigh mechanical assurance, and he had acquired aesthetic and theoretical principles, though these were subsequently to be subjected to extensive modifications. In short, Janáček was now a polished, solidly trained musician, with a technique certainly not inferior to that of the majority of his famous colleagues. It is important to grasp this fact since the legend of Janáček's contempt for technique, not to say inexperience or ignorance of the conventions of craftsmanship, is frequently proffered, and sometimes finds belief.

CHAPTER 4

CHORUSMASTER AND CRITIC
THE ORGAN SCHOOL AT BRNO
FIRST DIFFERENCES WITH PRAGUE

JANÁČEK'S RETURN to Brno was marked by a certain impatience and restlessness—the impulsive urge of a young creative artist who at long last wants to pursue his own path and test his strength. A number of stimulating tasks were awaiting him in Brno. Nearest to his heart was the development of a Czech national musical life in this town that was dominated by a German-speaking majority.

Compared with Prague, the Czech cultural life of Brno was in a rudimentary state. Petty provincialism paralysed the initiative of such cultural organisations as there were. In musical matters, particularly, a depressing dilettantism prevailed, which a lesser vitality than Janáček's would scarcely have been sufficient to overcome.

As a young teaching candidate Janáček had already deputised for the conductor of the male chorus *Svatopluk*, and had achieved some encouraging artistic successes with the society recruited from shop assistants and office workers. After his return from Prague in the autumn of 1875, he resumed his post as chorus master of the *Svatopluk* society. The letter in which he accepts the society's offer is a significant document of Janáček's youthful idealism.

'Respected committee of the co-operative society *Svatopluk* at Brno.

In consideration of the distressing social conditions of Brno in general, and of its musical life in particular, I am resolved unstintingly to apply all my powers wherever the ground is ready and the good will exists to uphold and further the cause of art. In choosing Brno as my first place of activity, I welcome the offer of your committee and accept it unreservedly in the interest of art and communal life. I have no other conditions to make.'[1]

With his dynamic vitality, Janáček soon made himself part of the Czech national musical life of Brno, and his efforts were those of an instigator, liberator and reformer. His capacity for work was astonishing. In February 1876, he took over the direction of the Beseda Brňenská choir, the leading musical institution of the Moravian capital. Apart from the interruptions caused by his stay in Leipzig and Vienna, he retained this post until the year 1888. He was now conductor of two renowned choral societies in Brno, apart from his paid appointment at the Teachers' Training College. And other obligations were to be added shortly.

Janáček's activity with the Beseda Brňenská choir throws a characteristic light on his talent for organisation and on the circumspection with which he approached any topical issue. In the first place, he strove to raise the artistic standards of the concerts. The 'glee-club' meetings with beer and band music and subsequent dancing generally preceded by some popular choruses and solo-numbers (these gatherings bore the characteristic name of 'conversational music') were gradually abolished and replaced by serious choral concerts. Out of the original male choir he created a mixed choir by admitting female voices, and he established an orchestra, at first consisting of amateur players; thus the society was now in a position to tackle larger choral works with orchestra. In the programmes of these concerts we find classical works such as Mozart's Requiem and Beethoven's Missa

[1]Undated; written probably after Janáček's return from Prague, 1875, when he was offered the unpaid post of deputy chorus master of the *Svatopluk* society. Cp. V. Helfert, Leoš Janáček, p. 206.

Solemnis, and also contemporary music, especially the compositions of Janáček's revered friend, Antonín Dvořák.

But Janáček's ideas extended further into the future. In order to secure fresh recruits for the orchestra of the Beseda, he proposed the founding of a Brno music school within the framework of the society. He gained his point, and in 1882, the original classes for strings were supplemented by courses for wind instruments and singing.

Janáček's vision, aiming at making Brno the musical centre of the country, became increasingly a reality. Notwithstanding the boldness of his ideas of organisation and reform, he always remained a realist who knew perfectly well that a flourishing concert life can only be guaranteed by first-class educational facilities. His artistic experiences in Prague, and even more, in Leipzig and Vienna, were now to bear fruit in Brno. In Prague, he had already conceived the plan of establishing an organ school in the Moravian capital. In order to realise this idea, he instigated in 1881 the foundation of a society for the promotion of church music in Moravia, and it was from this society that the Organ School arose in March, 1882. The Organ School was 'Janáček's creation and his pride', says Vladimír Helfert in his study of the composer.[1] Janáček devoted to it the best years of his pedagogic activity, and thus the institute became the training ground of a circle of students some of whom are still alive today and looking back with pride to their school days with the master.

From primitive, cramped and crowded beginnings, the Organ School developed into the leading musical teaching institute of Moravia. The curriculum was worked out by Janáček, and the full course, as in the Organ School at Prague, covered three years. The directorship was in Janáček's hands ; in addition, he taught theoretical subjects and composition to the third-year students.

[1] Cp. Vladimír Helfert, Leoš Janáček, p. 275.

He devoted himself with fatherly care to the instruction of his pupils and was no less concerned with their material well-being and their prospects of gaining secure employment. In his teaching of composition, the main accent was on the development of individual talent; originality was valued and new ideas encouraged. 'What matters is uncompromising truthfulness—in life as in art' was one of Janáček's maxims. His exposition was stimulating to the highest degree; imaginativeness, quick comprehension of a problem and its logical solution were the principles of his teaching. It may be that in Janáček's method of training, the strict, formal disciplines were given little scope; we know that polyphony and counterpoint were of secondary importance in his teaching of composition. His pupils loved and feared him—his fits of temper were notorious, but equally so his reconciliations and comradely affection.

Meanwhile, the curriculum of the Organ School was enlarged by the teaching of the other instrumental subjects. In the year 1906, the institute moved into its own splendid building in the Kounicová Street. The school house was graced by a classical portico, and in its garden, Janáček had built his own simple little house—a home among trees, which he loved, almost like a country house, yet at the same time in the middle of the town.

Thanks to his initiative, Brno now had two musical teaching institutes—the Organ School and the music school of the Beseda Society. The possibility of merging these two institutes occupied Janáček in the following years; but the plan was not to be realised until 1919, when the State Conservatoire was founded.

In the meantime, certain difficulties arose connected with Janáček's post at the Beseda. His insistence on a first-class musical standard met with the opposition of a group of members who were loth to forgo the former entertainments; moreover, he was criticised for propagating the works of Dvořák as also some compositions of his own. The crisis reached its climax in 1888, and Janáček, who was in any case becoming increasingly absorbed in his own creative work as a composer, curtly tendered his resignation from the committee of the Beseda.

Janáček's relation to Dvořák—an ardent admiration that lasted to the end of his life—and his attitude at this time to Smetana which was critical, not to say negative, are among the most interesting and psychologically revealing facets of his character. What drew him to Dvořák, who was his senior by thirteen years, was, apart from the typically Slavonic colour of the latter's music, the earthy, sensual, popular quality of his genius, the spontaneous and non-literary mould of his compositions; traits which he felt to be congenial with his own character but which, in Dvořák's case, had reached the stage of human and artistic maturity. Furthermore, Dvořák's classical principles agreed with the then classicistic ideas of Janáček. 'Do you know how it feels when someone else is taking the word from one's mouth? That is how Dvořák has taken his melodies from my heart.'[1] To be sure, this confession of Janáček sounds odd if one thinks of his mature art which arose from very different premises than those of Dvořák. But in Janáček's youthful works such as the *Suite for String Orchestra* (1877), the *Idyll* for String Orchestra (1878), or the opera *Šárka* (1887-88)[2] the influence of Dvořák was quite overwhelming.[3]

This attitude may serve to explain the fact that Janáček at that time considered Dvořák, not Smetana, to be the representative of Czech national music. 'I am convinced,' he said in a lecture on Czech folk song (March 1882), 'that we have in Antonín Dvořák our one and only Czech national composer.' In this remark, though it was dropped during the course of a probably unprepared

[1]Paul Stefan, *Anton Dvořák*, p. 84.

[2]The first of *Šárka's* four versions was examined by Dvořák, and on the basis of his criticism, Janáček had subjected the opera to a revision (second version). The third version is of the year 1918, the fourth of 1924.

[3]Janáček dedicated to Dvořák the *Four male choruses* (1885), the opera *Šárka* and the oratorio *Amarus* (1898).

address, the point against Smetana is unmistakable.

Janáček's attitude towards Smetana during the eighteen-seventies and early eighties was one of undisguised coolness, not to say active disapproval, which manifested itself in various astonishing gestures. One must not forget, however, that Smetana's position in the Czech camp was by no means incontestable at the time, and it seems that the negative attitude of Janáček and the Brno musical circles towards the composer of the *Bartered Bride* was a kind of echo of those animadversions to which Smetana was still to a certain extent exposed even in Prague.

At the time when Janáček held the directorship of the Beseda, Smetana's name was rarely found in the programmes of the society's concerts.[1] When the Brno Beseda was asked to commemorate the hundredth performance of the *Bartered Bride* (1882) by a contribution, the committee declined the proposal. Not until two years after Smetana's death was Brno ready to honour the memory of the master with a concert. But Janáček counselled against making a great occasion of it, and proposed the performance of a chorus and of the string quartet *From My Life*. The concert, which was insufficiently rehearsed, took place on April 18th, 1886; Janáček was unable to attend the ceremony because of illness.

In contrast to Janáček's attitude towards Smetana, his well-nigh unconditional allegiance to Dvořák is remarkable. The two musicians maintained a lively personal relationship. At one time, while Dvořák was away on a journey, Janáček lodged in his Prague apartments; in the summer of the same year (1883) they went together on a walking-tour of South Bohemia, on which they visited Dvořák's native village of Nelahozeves. On his frequent visits to Moravia, Dvořák was usually Janáček's guest.

[1] The reason Janáček subsequently gave for this was that Smetana's works belonged to the stage, whereas Dvořák's place was in the concert hall.

The composer and his young wife shortly after their wedding, 1881

Janáček with some of his pupils

portrait of the composer by Gustave Bohm, 1927

Under the influence of Janáček, a veritable Dvořák cult had come into being in Brno at the beginning of the eighteen-eighties. In April 1877, Janáček performed Dvořák's *Serenade for Strings*, in the next year there followed the *Moravian Duets*, four *Slavonic Dances* from the first, recently completed, series of these famous pieces[1] further, the *Slavonic Rhapsodies*, the *Czech Suite*, the *Symphonies* in F major, D major and A minor, the choral ballad *The Spectre's Bride* and the *Stabat Mater*. A rich selection, in comparison with which the repertoire of Smetana's works performed during the same time in Brno seems scant indeed.[2]

What were the reasons for this peculiar attitude of Janáček? It was certainly no personal prejudice that separated Janáček from Smetana. It was, in fact, the dissimilarity of Janáček's artistic personality, his Moravianess and arch-slavism, and not at least his peasant earthiness, which made him suspect the brilliant worldliness of Smetana. This eclectic composer, tending towards the music drama, opéra comique and the symphonic poem, the exponent of the New German School, was for Janáček the epitome of intellectually underpinned urbanity, of the bourgeois romanticism and modernism of Prague, and of the westernising trends of Bohemia in general. One must not forget that in the early eighties, Janáček was still adhering to classical, i.e. conservative tenets in art; thus, it is not surprising that he stood in the camp of Dvořák, the spiritual kinsman of Brahms. Later in life, however, Janáček acknowledged Smetana's mastery and integrity —'the lucid figure of Smetana will always be with us', was one of his sayings concerning the creator of the *Bartered Bride*.

This contradistinction opens yet another perspective: the rivalry between Prague and Brno, the capitals of Bohemia and Moravia, which came increasingly to the fore during the rebirth

[1]The orchestration of the first series of *Slavonic Dances* was completed by Dvořák on September 22nd, 1878.

[2]In December 1880 and March 1883, Smetana's symphonic poem *Vetava*, and in March 1886, *Vyšehrad* were performed. Besides, single pieces by Smetana appeared in the programmes of the Beseda in the years 1883, 1884 and 1886.

of the Czech nation. A certain patronising centralism on the part of Prague had at all times given offence in Brno, and the fact that the musical 'establishment' in Prague in their publication *Dalibor* minimised, or altogether ignored, Janáček's plans of reform gave the latter an added reason for insisting on the separateness and autonomy of Moravia's national renaissance as distinct from that of Bohemia.

One of Janáček's resources in his task of construction was the musical journal *Hudební Listy* which he founded in 1884. He was by no means inexperienced as a critic and writer. For some time, he had been the music critic of the daily paper *Moravská Orlice*, and had come to know the educational value of factual reporting. In *Hudební Listy*, he advocated above all, the creation of a Czech national theatre in Brno.[1] In numerous aesthetical and historical articles, he gave expression to his artistic ideas; through his reviews of contemporary music, however, he became involved in polemics which were to have far-reaching effects.

Janáček's belligerent spirit and the ingenuousness of his convictions and prejudices came strongly to the fore now. His articles and reviews reflect his prevailing artistic views, his faith in the national basis of the new Czech music, his rejection of virtuosity and extraneousness, his demand for simplicity, sincerity and technical solidity.[2] And it was in the columns of the *Hudební Listy* that the first skirmishes of the subsequent battle for the recognition of his works in Prague were fought. One of the contributors was Karel Kovařovič (1862-1920), the Prague composer and future operatic conductor of the Prague National Theatre.[3] With his usual, incorruptible straightforwardness,

[1] The beginnings of an independent Czech theatre in Brno go back to the eighteen seventies.

[2] In a criticism of a concert in which Janáček himself took part as a pianist, he writes: 'Your correspondent confirms that Mr. Janáček in his improvisation merely played what came under his fingers. This is indeed quite unforgivable. The general impression of the concert left much to be desired.'

[3] From 1885 to 1886 conductor of the Czech theatre at Brno, from 1900 musical director of the Prague National Theatre.

Janáček had in *Hudební Listy* given an adverse criticism to a new opera of Kovařovič, *The Betrothed* (*Ženichové*), and this, regardless of the fact that Kovařovič had recently written in the same paper an enthusiastic account of a jubilee concert given by the Beseda. There was a sharp retort to Janáček's review in the Prague *Dalibor*, to which Janáček replied in his turn. This journalistic episode, so characteristic for his upright, combative nature, greatly contributed to the worsening of the already strained relations between Prague and Brno. A few years later, Janáček was to experience the full, dire consequences of this incident.

Other polemics followed, mostly about Smetana's operas and their musico-dramatic style; a great many fundamental questions were raised, concerning which the opinions of *Hudební Listy* and *Dalibor* differed profoundly. In this controversy between Janáček's formalism and the late-romantic principles that were upheld by *Dalibor*, Janáček cannot be entirely exonerated from the reproach of obstinacy. However cogently he tried to rationalise his critical objections to Smetana, the fact remains that in those days Janáček could or would not understand the formal and melodic-harmonic principles of the New German School. It was certainly unwise of him to use his prejudices as weapons against artistic concepts that were alien to him, and it was in the nature of the given situation that he should lose the first phases of this battle. But the price he had to pay for his refusal to yield was high. He had spoilt his chances with Prague for years to come; things even reached a point where he was not taken seriously as a musician in Prague. In particular, it was the Kovařovič episode which, when Janáček offered his *Jenufa* for performance at the Bohemian capital, brought about one of the greatest crises of his career.

CHAPTER 5

UNDER THE SPELL OF FOLK MUSIC

'I FEEL that my present works are failures; I write them, as it were, in an iron suit of armour—how long will I have to struggle again to shed this repression of my true self.'[1] Janáček wrote these words in one of those moments of self-analysis which now became more and more frequent with him. They are the signs of a new crisis in his development; a crisis, this time, which betokened a profound change in his spiritual personality.

During the eighteen-eighties, a decisive revolution took place in Janáček's artistic development. As with most long-lived artists, his arrival at full maturity was preceded by a relatively lengthy period of preparation. It was not until he had reached the middle of his third decade that he became conscious of his true goals, and even so, another twenty years had to elapse before his first masterpiece *Jenufa* was completed.

The break-through of his genius swept away former attachments and restrictions, and the young artist was filled by a new vision of his mission. He now recognised that it was by origin and race that his art should be nurtured. As a Czech patriot, he therefore retreated from the political conservatism of his youth, which was strongly influenced by the clerical nationalism of his convent education. The spirit of liberalism took hold of him more

[1]From a letter, written in German, to Zdenka Schulz, Leipzig, 1880.

and more, and Janáček's nationalism, combative and passionate as ever, moved now in an artistically as well as socially progressive direction. His interest in church music declined steadily; ritual and politico-religious considerations seemed to him incompatible with his artistic demand for a modern church music that should be independent of traditional clichés. Realising more and more that his gifts lay in another direction, he gradually renounced his old classical and formalistic ideas. His whole interest was now concentrated on folk song and language with its thousandfold nuances of expression and cadence. With the usual intensity of his artistic convictions and searching intelligence, he now plunged into the study of folk music and of the musical elements contained in language. From these sources, his genius drew that freedom which, as a man and artist, was to lead him onto a new path. An enhanced feeling of passionate uncompromise now takes possession of him: Janáček stands on the threshold of his very own art with its realism, social commitment and inspiration drawn from the people.

On the 15th of August 1882, his first child, Olga, was born. The choice of her Christian name, as also that of his son, Vladimír, born six years later (16 May, 1888, died 9 November, 1890), reflects his Russophilism, which was certainly not the product of some sentimental panslavistic attitude, but rested on quite practical reasoning.[1] His children became a deep source of happiness to him. In little Vladimír, he discovered signs of musical talent; the more terrible was the blow of the boy's sudden death. Janáček never really recovered from this loss.

In spite of these family ties, there occurred at that time a serious estrangement from his wife. Zdenka's German origin and urban, middle-class education—and probably her youthful inexperience

[1] 'Our well-being lies with the East, not with the West. The Slavonic East needs us, while we are superfluous to the Germanic and Romanic West.' From an article published in the Moravská Orlice, 1867. The ideas expressed in the above quotation were general property among Czech patriots in those days, and, no doubt, also part of Janáček's own national convictions.

as well—produced in Janáček an unbearable irritation which was
coming to a head just at the time of Olga's birth. Janáček left
Zdenka and did not return to his family for two years. This was
the first crisis in his marriage, and it broke in with a directness
and fury that can only be understood if one takes into consideration the general, profound changes that were taking place in
Janáček's personality. Zdenka and the middle-class atmosphere
of her home were a kind of symbol of Janáček's former development. With the awakening of his national consciousness, he
ceased to rely on these social safeguards. Zdenka's patrician origin
and Janáček's former artistic conservatism were psychologically
very closely allied. As he was shaking off the latter, his attitude
to society and to his wife's personality was bound to undergo
a transformation.

Janáček relates in his memoirs that in 1879 he began to study
the inflections of speech and the musical motifs—'speech-
motifs' (nápěvky)—derived from these. 'The inflections of
human speech and indeed of the voices of all creatures became
to me a source of profound truth—a life-necessity, as it were . . .
Speech-motifs are my windows into the soul . . . they are the
expression of a being's totality and of all phases of its activity.'[1]
Speech-motifs were valued by Janáček as true-to-life formulae
descriptive of states of the mind; as such, they became the
starting point, the raw material, as it were, of his vocal and
dramatic music. 'It was so strange. It happened that, when someone spoke to me, I did not always understand his words, but I did
understand the melodic cadences of his speech. I knew at once
whether that person lied or was inwardly agitated; sometimes,
during a most ordinary conversation, I felt, and indeed heard,
that my interlocutor was inwardly weeping.'[2]

This extreme sensitivity towards the musico-psychological

[1]From an essay of Janáček in the journal *Loni a letos*, 1905.
[2]From an interview, 1928.

expressiveness of speech had no doubt been sharpened by Janáček's interest in folk song, in which he discovered an analogous law applying to the linguistic-musical projection of spontaneous sensations. For Janáček, folk song was not so much a stylised form, adapted to suit conventional musical sensibility, as a vital ebullience, a heartfelt outcry, a jubilation, a plaint—and it was in its variety of mood and its elemental naturalness that folk song touched upon speech-motifs.

Janáček's retreat from classical conventions and the gradual transformation of his artistic orientation went hand in hand with his deep-rooted nationalism. Folk song and speech-inflection became now the fundaments of his musical thinking—surely the most vital national media for an artist of Janáček's constitution.

He had begun to collect folk songs in 1885. On his frequent visits to his uncle, the curate of the village Znorov in Eastern Moravia, he had come to know the bitter-sweet charm of the music of these simple countryfolk. He was fascinated by the tonal, harmonic and rhythmic peculiarities of their songs and dances. Soon, his folkloristic researches took him to other parts of Moravia and Silesia, to Velká, near the Slovakian border, and above all to his native Hukvaldy. At Velká, a village with unspoilt folkloristic traditions, he made friends with the folk singer Martin Zeman (the 'bearded' Martin Zeman, as Janáček called him), and in Hukvaldy he discussed with the game-keeper Sládeček not only the linguistic progress of the latter's little daughter, but also the fascinating sounds and calls of the forest animals. The Lachian and Wallachian idiom of Janáček's native folk music characterises the *Lachian Dances* (1889-90), the *Folk Poetry of Hukvaldy in Songs* (*Ukvalská lidová poesie v písních*, 1898) and the *Folk Songs of Hukvaldy* (*Ukvalské písně*, 1899).

In those days, Janáček came into close contact with the well-known Moravian folklorist František Bartoš (1837-1906), the editor of two comprehensive collections of Moravian folk songs.

Bartoš, to be sure, approached the problem of notating and setting the songs from a different angle than Janáček. Romantic idealisation and stylisation reigns supreme in his versions of the texts as well as the melodies, and it was Janáček's main task in his collaboration with Bartoš to steer a middle course, if no more, in the selection and treatment of the material. For Bartoš' collection *Moravian Folk Songs* (*Moravské lidové písné*, 1889), Janáček wrote a short introduction dealing with the musical character of the melodies; subsequently (1901) he edited together with Bartoš the monumental anthology of Moravian folk songs that was to be published in Prague under the patronage of the Czech Academy of Sciences and Arts.

In his notation of folk songs, Janáček was by no means content with adapting the melodies to conventional tonal and rhythmical schemes, such as was customary in the middle of the Nineteenth Century. He was aiming at an entirely realistic reproduction of the songs and their manner of performance. In the melodic and harmonic peculiarities of folk songs, and particularly in their frequent modality and unorthodox modulations, Janáček saw the manifestation of a mature musical tradition and, generally speaking, the expression of the manifold forms of a nation's life. But the rhythmical felicities, especially, were carefully registered by Janáček. The frequently irregular metres were noted down, and the tempo of the melody and duration of its single notes measured with the aid of watch and metronome. In later years, Janáček employed the recently invented phonograph and a sensitive chronoscope.[1]

With scientific detachment he classified the melodies into various types. He distinguishes 'expanded' folk songs, particularly those where the final syllables are drawn out (*Songs of Hukvaldy*), and dance songs. Again, he establishes four types of the latter.

[1]"There is something invigorating, something shimmering and shadowy in rhythm; something that does not agree with the dry registration of the time units by the metronome. Ah, these hemi-demi-semi-hemi-demi-semiquavers'! From a note of Janáček's.

In his numerous essays on folk music, Janáček proves himself a keen observer with a clear, analytical eye; but above all else, he is an artist to whom songs and lays have opened an inexhaustible source of life and inspiration.

Next to the folk song, Janáček gave his attention to folk dancing. He studied the choreography of the various dance forms in the villages, and went so far as to learn the art of the czimbalon[1] and bagpipe players. The rhapsodic character of folk dance accompaniments greatly influenced Janáček's instrumental music.[2] As he found in Fr. Bartoš a congenial collaborator for his folk song studies, so he obtained the cooperation of the Brno folk dance expert Lucie Bakesŏvá for his choreographic researches. The fruit of his interest in the choreographic aspect of folk dancing was the ballet *Rákocz Rákoczy*, a series of rustic dance scenes on a libretto of Jan Herben, in which Janáček used some of his *Lachian Dances* and Hanakian dancing songs, combining these with a mixed chorus and solo voices. The work was successfully performed at the Prague National Theatre in July 1891; from that time, Janáček was considered principally a folklorist.

All these experiences bore rich fruit in the composer's career. On the occasion of the ethnological exhibition held in 1895 in Prague, he was entrusted with organising the folkloristic contributions of Moravia. The rural choirs and dancing groups from Velká and other villages in their many-coloured costumes, and with their traditional instruments were highlights of the exhibition. Here, Janáček became acquainted with the folklorist and Smetana-expert Otakar Hostinský (1847-1910); a friendship which was to lead to the collaboration of the two men on many important tasks.

It is evident that Janáček's development as a musician and folklorist was bound to have characteristic repercussions on his own

[1]Belonging to the dulcimer family and frequently used both as an accompanying and solo instrument, chiefly in Hungarian, Slovakian, Roumanian and Yugoslav folk music.
[2]cf. Chapter 9.

compositions. While the compositions of his Leipzig and Vienna
time are in the main based on formalistic principles, albeit with
a strong admixture of the late-romantic idiom, we find that,
with his early male choruses, he has suddenly entered his own
domain. Some of these are settings of folk songs, such as *Ploughing*
(*Orání*, 1873), and *How Strange My Lover Is* (*Divím se milému*,
1875-6), but most of them are original settings of folk song texts—
vigorous, harsh, in the spirit of Moravian and Slovak folk music,
exemplified, among others, by *True Love* (*Láska opravdivá*, 1876),
Inconstant Love (*Nestálost lásky*, 1873), *You Will not Escape Fate*
(*Osudu neujdeš*, 1878), *O Love* (*O lásko*, 1885). It is highly characteristic of Janáček that he found in folk music the key to his
personal, realistic style. It was through the study of folk song and
speech-melody that his idiom gained that vocal aspect which
henceforth was to characterise his work, including his instrumental
music.

It is surprising that Janáček should not have reset or re-modelled
a greater number of existing folk songs. The reason seems to be
that most of the traditional folk tunes were, in Janáček's opinion,
not doing full justice to the emotional content of their words.
His usual procedure was, therefore, to clothe the texts of folk
songs in his own music, while using some melodic turns contained in their tunes. Frequently, however, he entirely disregards
the given melodic material, and fully re-composes the texts. Some
of his best and most gripping choruses were in this category, as
for instance *War, War* (*Ach, vojna*, 1885), and *Warning* (*Výhrůžka*,
1885), in fact the whole group of the *Four Male Choruses* which he
dedicated to Antonín Dvořák in 1886.

Janáček's reluctance to introduce folk song elements in his
works must be regarded as a further token of his artistic independence. Himself a son of that mysterious, primal power called 'the
people', he was not constrained to quote existing melodies. 'Every
composer,' he once wrote, 'has a claim to the spirit of folk song;

but he has no claim to the work of another who creates in the spirit of folk song. Every folk song, after all, has been composed by someone. The fact that the composer is not named does not give anyone the right to appropriate it. Enough has been taken from our people already without this being asked'. It is for this reason that Janáček subsequently repudiated his opera *Beginning of a Romance* (*Počátek románu*) (1894) in which Moravian folk songs are quoted.

Janáček, the man of the people and born dramatist, became increasingly aware of his real vocation during those formative years; from now on it was opera, the realistic drama springing from the source of popular sentiment, which principally claimed his interest.

Leoš Janáček was thirty years old when he wrote his first opera, *Šárka* (1887-88). The reason for his delay in embarking on his proper career is doubtless to be found in the emphasis in his education on classical and church music, but probably also in the primitive cultural conditions in Brno, which until the year 1884 had no Czech stage. He had, however, considered the writing of a dramatic work even before the inception of *Šárka*, for there is an entry in his diary for 1885 in which he noted down the action of Chateaubriand's *Les Aventures du Dernier des Abencérages*.[1]

In *Šárka*, Janáček once more explored the means of expression hitherto employed by him; with the result, that the opera remained an uneven experiment in spite of radical revision later. The fact that he chose to compose this legend of Julius Zeyer with its surfeit of mythological symbolism is in itself an indication of Janáček's as yet uncertain taste and lack of direction as a dramatic composer. Since he had omitted to ask the poet for permission to set his text to music, Zeyer prohibited the performance of the opera. Thus, the work had to wait a long time to

[1] Cherubini's opera *Les Abencérages* is of the year 1813. Janáček had heard the overture of this work at a concert in Leipzig.

come before the public, and even in its revised form of 1924[1] it failed to make a convincing impression.

A few years after the disappointing Šárka episode, Janáček, who was still searching for a truly popular operatic subject, hit upon a rustic drama by Gabriella Preissová *Beginning of a Romance* (Počátek Románu). A light and shallow versification by Jaroslav Tichý served the composer as a basis for music that was written in the vein of light opera, representing, as it did, a further phase in the evolution of Janáček the dramatist. The work was completed in the late autumn of 1891. On the strength of his Prague success with the ballet *Rákocz Rákoczy*, the composer hoped that this opera would be accepted by the Prague National Theatre. However, after a correspondence with the intendant F. A. Šubert, that lasted for the better part of two years, he had to resign himself to the rejection of the opera. Performed in 1894 at Brno, the unassuming work had quite a friendly reception.

Janáček himself criticised this youthful opera more severely than was justified in view of its qualities. 'Beginning of a Romance was an empty comedy. My inexperience led me to use folk songs in it,' was Janáček's later comment about the work. In fact, it was the dramatic counterpart to the pantomime tableau *Rákocz Rákoczy*; a play with songs, a necessary experience for the folk-lorist Janáček, who, when faced with this dramatic stage work, began to realise for the first time what the true spirit of a modern, realistic popular opera should be. His next work for the stage, *Jenufa*, was to prove the value of this lesson.

[1]Janáček's pupil Osvald Chlubna had undertaken most of the revision, and had re-orchestrated the third act.

CHAPTER 6

THE STRUGGLE FOR JENUFA

JANÁČEK WAS nearly fifty years old when, on the 18th of March 1903, he completed the score of *Jenufa*, or *Her Ward* (*Její Pastorkyně*), to give the opera its official title. A few weeks before (the 27th of February, 1903), he had lost his daughter Olga in her twenty-first year. The threat of this catastrophe, which had been hanging over Janáček for many months, and the emotional situation presented in Acts II and III of the opera, which were written at that time, have a certain similarity: anxiety about the life of a child, and despair and helplessness once the blow has fallen. Janáček's almost fanatical hope of saving the life of his daughter and his confidence in the opera's acceptance by the Prague National Theatre had utterly collapsed within the space of a few months. There is a strange inner connection between the completion of *Jenufa* and the fate of Olga; an unconscious psychological equation between the creative artist and the father, who, as it were, fears for the existence of the two beings that are so much a part of his life and who, as soon as both are lost, finds himself face to face with one of the gravest crises of his life.

The years during which *Jenufa* was created are marked by a strange restlessness and passion on the part of Janáček. It is as if the composer was being taken out of his usual life and habitually rational conduct, and transported to a loftier, more inspired sphere that revealed to him new resources of strength and taught him the obligation of living henceforth for his creative activity alone. Thus, at a time when the success of his compositions was by no means assured, he tendered his resignation from the Teachers' Training College in Brno (October 1904). Shortly before, he had declined the offer of the directorship of the Warsaw Conservatoire; not so much because the conditions he made were found unacceptable, but because he felt that he should devote his energies to the creative work that had to be done in his homeland. The more his studies of speech melody deepened his insight into the human soul, and indeed enhanced the orbit of his humanity, the more profoundly was he shaken by the irrevocable deterioration of Olga who at that time—in the early summer of 1902—stayed with Janáček's brother František in St. Petersburg. 'Your whole sad story is now quite clear to me. Do not distress yourself by brooding over your illness, and try not to lose your confidence. . . . With what anguish I am asking for news from you! My life is a much heavier burden to me than you know. Only get well, my girl! My thoughts are with you . . . My poor child, how you have to suffer . . .' Janáček was trembling for the life of the only child fate had left him. Do we not feel in the anxious imprecations of this letter the feverish worry of Jenufa about her child, her uncanny presentiment of an imminent catastrophe? This influx of a personal factor from Janáček's life into the world of *Jenufa* was subsequently admitted by the composer in these words: 'I should like to drape *Jenufa* in the shroud of the long illness, the pains and anguish of my daughter Olga and my little boy Vladimír.' He dedicated the work to the memory of Olga.

Janáček was fully aware of the particular artistic value of his *Jenufa*. This work had been created out of the fullness of his artistic and human experience. No forerunner of something that was to be achieved; it was achievement itself—strong and self-respecting—a first fulfilment. Therefore Janáček intended the

THE STRUGGLE FOR 'JENUFA'   63

opera to reach the public only by way of an artistically flawless
performance on a front-rank stage. The Prague Czech National
Theatre was such a stage, and the composer submitted his score
in the spring of 1903, shortly after its completion.

To be sure, Janáček had unnecessarily prejudiced, not to say
jeopardised, his position in Prague by his former polemics (cp.
Ch. 4), and in particular by his clash with Karel Kovařovič, who
was at the time the influential musical director of the National
Theatre. The rejection of *Jenufa* by Kovařovič was therefore the
logical result of previous discordances. Janáček was hit very hard
by this decision, which shook his confidence in himself as an
artist and paralysed his creative power for several months. The
crisis precipated by the death of Olga was further aggravated by
the fact that soon after, Janáček's relations with his wife Zdenka
began to deteriorate seriously.

But Janáček was not the man to break down under the blows
of fate, however cruel they might be. During the course of that
year—in October 1903, to be precise—*Jenufa* was accepted for
performance by the director of the Czech Theatre in Brno. The
première of the opera took place on the 21st of January, 1904, and
was a triumphant success, if only of provincial standing. Seen
from Brno, this performance was a national event, and perspica-
cious critics already held the correct assessment of this new figure
in the realm of Czech music who was destined, side by side with
Smetana, if not beyond him, to secure for Czech opera a place
in the musico-dramatic world repertoire.

Prague musical circles, however, remained closed to the
composer from the Moravian province. But one should not
forget that Janáček was known in the Bohemian capital chiefly
as a folklorist; as the composer of the ballet *Rákocz Rákoczy*
and the opera *Beginning of a Romance*, both works which draw
liberally on folk melodies. Besides, Janáček had been Fr. Bartoš'
collaborator in the latter's collection of folk songs. Janáček's

artistic principles of composition were recognised as original, but his music was considered primitive and offending in many ways against the canons of good taste, national tradition and theatrical convention. His efforts to eliminate certain dramatic shortcomings of the opera, to improve the orchestration, to excise redundant passages were in vain.[1] The fact that Janáček during those years did not lose faith in his artistic mission, and indeed was capable of creating further masterpieces (above all, the male choruses on the texts of Peter Bezruč), is a token of his inner strength and of the vitality of his creativity. In Prague, his chances seem to be gone for ever. It is true that some of his choral works among them *Maryčka Magdonová*, and the cantata *Our Father (Otče náš)* were performed with success, and that the orchestral piece *Jealousy (Žarlivost)*, a concert revision of the overture to *Jenufa*, was played under František Neumann (1904). However, to the operatic composer Janáček, the Bohemian capital remained inaccessible.

'Janáček has as many enemies in Prague as he has hairs on his head. They know quite well who he is—hence their hatred'— thus a critic wrote at the time to Dr. František Veselý, one of the most active friends of the composer. Dr. Veselý was president of the *Association of the Friends of Art in Moravia*. Together with his wife, Marie Calma Veselá, a gifted singer and writer, he led for several years the struggle towards the recognition of Janáček's works, and especially of *Jenufa*, in Prague. It would take too long to describe in detail the numerous endeavours and interventions by which the Veselýs sought to further the cause of Janáček. Kovařovič, in whose hands lay the decision of accepting an opera for the National Theatre, remained intransigent. In his judgment of the opera, which had been submitted to him in full score, he recognised the quality of some of the monologues,

---

[1]The revisions of *Jenufa* occurred in the years 1906 and 1911, and particularly before the Prague première of 1916.

The National Theatre at Brno

former Organ School at Brno with the garden entrance (left) to Janáček's small villa

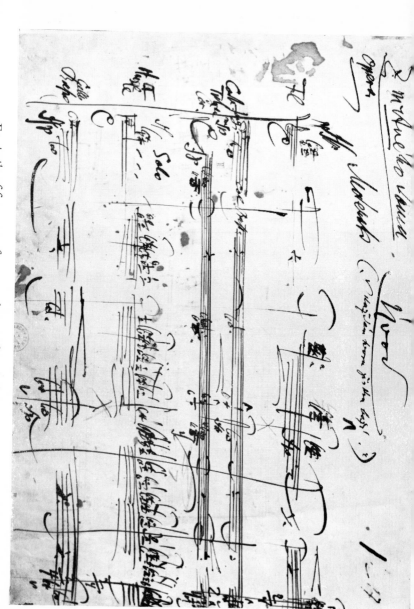

Facsimile of fragment of autograph score from 'The House of the Dead'

but found the dialogues most unsatisfactory, chiefly because of the frequent repetitions of words; altogether, he maintained that the work was lacking in any stylistic unity, and that it was 'a mixture of attempts directed towards a forced novelty of style, of extreme primitivism that bordered on artistic incapacity, and of lapses into a long since surmounted atavism.'[1] But Maria Calma did not yield. She sang various parts from *Jenufa* in private circles, and among her listeners, many of whom were influential people, the conviction gradually gained ground that the Prague public was being deprived of a masterpiece. In the late autumn of 1915, eleven years after the Brno première, Kovařovič withdrew his opposition. He had at long last been persuaded by the beauty and the dramatic effectiveness of *Jenufa*, and he promised to conduct the opera himself the next spring. However, there remained certain reservations. Janáček had to agree to various cuts and changes in the orchestration in order that 'the work may gain in tension and flow and its dramatic impact be heightened'.[2] One of the cuts was concerned with the exit of the guardian in Act I; there were omissions in Laca's scene, and the repetition of single words and sentences was in many places eliminated. All in all, these alterations were really to the good, and they scarcely affected the dramatic construction of the three acts. The orchestration, which in parts had been too thin, was improved by doublings; above all, the final scene was lent more colour by a more effective entry of the brass (trumpets and imitatory work in the horns), whose brilliant and solemn tone, it is said, moved Janáček to tears at one of the Prague *Jenufa* rehearsals.

The Prague première of *Jenufa* took place on the 26th of May, 1916. The work was received with unprecedented enthusiasm, in which, to be sure, was contained a strong dose of demonstrative nationalism. Janáček's name was the centre of all discussions. The

[1] From a letter of G. Schmoranz, director of the Prague National Theatre, to the critic K. Sipek.

[2] Kovařovič's words, quoted in a letter of Dr. F. Veselý to Janáček.

reviews were, for the most part, positive; his position as a composer was compared to that of Smetana; his dramatic realism, his affinity with the people, his lyrical invention were commented upon from every angle. But there were also critical voices. Thus, the well-known Smetana expert, Prof. Zdeněk Nejedlý complained of the 'unfeasibility and lifelessness' of Janáček's style, of his lack of ethnographical truth (sic:), of the 'involuntary humour' that is produced by his repetitions of words—which we know to be poetically and psychologically well-founded—and, in general, of the inartistic 'naturalism' of Janáček's melodic invention.

At the age of sixty-two, Leoš Janáček stood now at the zenith of his fame, and quite certainly held the foremost place in the ranks of contemporary Czech composers. Soon, the question of a German performance of *Jenufa* was raised, and it happened in this connection that, through the agency of the composer Josef Suk, Janáček came into contact with the Prague *littérateur* Max Brod, whose sensitive understanding of Janáček's art, coupled with great linguistic adaptability, made him an ideal translator for most of the operas[1] and vocal works of the Moravian master. In Brod's congenial translation, *Jenufa* set out on its triumphant course on the German stage. As a gesture of political goodwill, the Vienna Court Opera presented on the 18th of February 1918, a memorable performance of the work, splendidly produced and sung, and even attended by members of the Austrian Imperial House. The title role was sung by Marie Jeritza, the part of the guardian by Lucie Weidt; Hugo Reichenberger was the conductor. There followed Berlin (1924), New York (1924) and other theatres over the world. The international success of *Jenufa* and its creator was assured.

At the time in question two women received letters from

[1] Of Janáček's operas, Max Brod translated *Jenufa*, *Káťá Kabanová*, *The Cunning Little Vixen*, *The Makropulos Case*, and *The House of the Dead*. The translator of *The Excursions of Mr. Brouček* was Otto Sonnenfeld.

Janáček in which the composer describes his impressions of the days of *Jenufa's* Vienna triumph. 'How I should like to have you with me—you have no idea what is happening to me. Today, there was a rehearsal (at the Vienna Court Opera), already in costumes. The designs and the lighting were as for a performance. The colours, the hundred-and-fifty costumes, the marvellous deep stage, everything in new splendour . . . Sunshine of a kind that even the spectator might begin to sweat . . . Frau Weidt acts excellently . . . She is a soprano, so she has not your silky, dark voice that is so suitable to the action . . . You must see it . . .' These lines were addressed to Gabriela Horvátová, the Prague singer of the guardian in *Jenufa* with whom Janáček had in those days formed an intimate friendship. In another letter he says: 'Since my Vienna days I have again been to the place, and have returned from Prague today. Great jealousy has arisen between Vienna and Prague over the question as to which performance is the better one. Well, though it's not so sumptuous, it is cosier at home. Believe me, I became so excited by everything that I am longing for some peace now . . .' The recipient of this communication was Kamilla Stoesslová, the wife of a merchant in the Moravian town of Přerov (later in Písek). Janáček had met her in 1915 at Hukvaldy. In the summer of 1917 the two married couples spent some time at the Moravian spa of Luhačovice, and these holiday weeks formed the beginning of the composer's close relationship with this woman who was his junior by thirty-eight years.

Temperamentally, Kamilla Stoesslová was very different from Janáček's wife. Zdenka, the woman of patrician origin, German mother-tongue, distinguished, urban, upper middle-class tastes and restrained character, became a lonely, embittered woman during the composer's last years of life. He had never been able to resolve the conflict that was engendered by his peasant origin, Slav nationalism and compassion for the socially underprivileged.

On the other hand, the demonic side of Janáček's nature, which early on had frightened Zdenka, was never psychologically assimilated by her. The tragedy of her position became particularly acute as her husband's relation to Kamilla Stoesslová developed into an overpowering passion that silenced all other considerations. The robustness and gaiety, the true feminity and sensuous warmth of Kamilla's temperament entirely captivated the ageing man. Under the enchantment of this relationship, Janáček was to create the most glowing works of his late maturity; the operas *Kátà Kabanová*, *The Cunning Little Vixen*, *The House of the Dead*, *The Diary of a Young Man who Vanished*, the *Glagolitic Mass* and the *Second String Quartet*.

CHAPTER 7

THE MASTER

THE PRAGUE triumph of *Jenufa*, as well as the closely following political uprising of 1918 which gave the Czech people their national independence, had the happiest effect on the last years of Janáček's life. With the serenity and self-assurance of a victor he stands now at the peak of his career. Beloved of his friends and feared by his enemies, he had grown into a national figure—not because he had modified his revolutionary ideas, a thing impossible to him—but because the Czech people, thanks to their own historic past, really understood these revolutionary principles and, in point of fact, actually lived up to them in their social and political institutions. Add to this that the wholesome popular realism of Janáček's art, his Russophilism, and not least the ethical ideals of his philosophy, derived, as it were, from the Slavonic emotional sphere, formed an ideal complement to the political realism and Western democratic humanism of T. G. Masaryk, the first president of the Czechoslovak republic. Thus, Janáček's position as a national artist was organically united with the national destiny and the national triumph of 1918.

Janáček, who had been able to wait for success so long, did not assume that his victory gave him the right to rest and inactivity. On the contrary, his participation in, and feeling of responsibility towards the cultural problems of the young state were livelier than ever, and his creative powers were to inspire him during his last years to write some of his most significant masterpieces.

As at the time of his struggle for recognition, he again saw in his success a challenge and an obligation. As soon as the new order of things was beginning to function, he did not hesitate to raise his voice. And here again, it is in the first place the reformer and organiser who makes himself heard. In November 1918, a few weeks after the establishment of the new state, Janáček submitted to the Prague authorities a scheme recommending the transformation of the Brno Organ School into a State Conservatoire. The petition was granted, and Janáček was provided with a special position by the founding of a master-class for composition. Janáček was professor of this master-class at the Brno Conservatoire from September 1919 to February 1925. It is characteristic that this highest institute of musical education in Moravia was administratively dependent on the Prague Conservatoire. However, the generation of Janáček's pupils who had the benefit of his tuition and friendship, has always, and with good reason, been considered a group of *Moravian* artists.[1]

Above everything else, Janáček gave his attention to the musical life of Brno. Through the transfer of the former German Theatre into Czech hands, the Czech musical life of Brno gained a stage which was large enough to satisfy the requirements of a modern opera and also to house a full symphony orchestra. It was due to Janáček's initiative that, given these premises, regular philharmonic concerts were instituted. Though he himself rarely appeared as conductor, these concerts were the fulfilment of his dream of placing the concert life of the Moravian capital on a representative level. Through the recommendation of the Master, František Neumann was engaged (1919), and Brno acquired an

[1]Among Janáček's pupils were Břetislav Bakala, Osvald Chlubna, Pavel Haas, Václav Kapral, Jan Kunc, Jaroslav Kvapil, Vilém Petrželka.

experienced and modern-minded conductor, under whose direction the Philharmonic Concerts, and above all, the opera, entered
upon a brilliant era. In the musically eventful third decade of the
century, the Brno National Theatre, in collaboration with the
gifted producer Ota Zitek, mounted no less than six first performances of Janáček's operas.[1] Notwithstanding certain restrictions,
the Brno stage has to this day retained what is in fact the authentic
style of Janáček's operas.[2]

In the cultivation of chamber music, too, Janáček's influence
was vitalising. Under his auspices, the *Society of Moravian
Composers* was founded in 1922, a body that took for its task the
fostering of native, and also of international chamber music.
Directly and indirectly, this society strongly promoted the per-
forming of Janáček's chamber music works. For three years
the master held the position of president in the conviction that
'whatever one may have needed me for at first' was no longer
topical—'every one of you will ripen now under his own sun'[3]—
he resigned in November, 1925, from this honorary position.

In the streets of Brno, in the concert hall and theatre, Janáček's
dynamic figure could not be overlooked. On a thickset body
sat a marvellous head whose powerful forehead was crowned by
dense white hair. Unforgettable were his eyes which could
become dreamy or passionate; two dark, restless flames, seemed
to penetrate to the ultimate source of things. His terse, eruptive
speech was accompanied by sudden temperamental gestures;
these were also characteristic of his gait which was jaunty and
short-paced as with someone in a hurry who avoids any
unnecessary delay.

His study in the half-hidden little house standing in the garden
of the Organ School was of the utmost simplicity. A large

[1] *Šárka* (1925), *The Excursions of Mr. Brouček* (1920), *Kátà Kabanová* (1921), *The Cunning
Little Vixen* (1924), *The Makropulos case* (1926), *The House of the Dead* (1930).
[2] Janáček once declared: 'I have seen my works in international houses, but I must say
that Neumann does them best of all.'
[3] From a letter to the *Society of Moravian Composers*: 23rd November, 1925.

Ehrbar grand piano, littered with books and manuscripts, gave a professional air to the room. There was a photo of Dvořák on the desk; a picture of Smetana, however, was missing in Janáček's house. The visual arts did not mean much to this man of the people. An exception were the Moravian-Slovakian peasant crafts, which Janáček looked at with the eye of the folklorist, and with which he liked to surround himself. His home was adorned by richly ornamented, embroidered cloths, brightly painted plates and jugs, and similar pieces of furniture. His reading comprised (apart from contemporary Czech authors) a number of French works (Corneille, Racine, Molière), and above all, Russian dramas and novels, which he read in the original. For a time, he even tried to come to grips with Einstein's theory of relativity. 'But his relativity of time and space is inapplicable to sound', he wrote to Max Brod. 'We live by air, not by ether. We smell the earth. But then, we stand firmly on it.'

The little white house at the back of the Organ School and the primitive peasant cottage which Janáček bought at Hukvaldy gave him peace and the environment he needed for his creative work. Every summer, he spent several weeks at his native village in the Eastern Moravian hills. Here, he went for long tramps through the familiar forests: there, he sat 'under the pear tree' in the garden, listening to the voices of nature; here he composed and flourished in the homely, God-given peace of the countryside. He was on terms of friendship with many villagers, as for instance, the keeper Sládeček who, like the composer, knew all about animals' voices. As with Dvořák, Janáček loved the earth and particularly the hardy soil of his homeland and its simple, raw people; and even when he was acclaimed by the great world, his longing went out to the Hukvaldy forests which were able to renew his vital and creative energies.

Janáček's Slavonic allegiances, fortified by the new political situation, drew him once again into the orbit of Russian literature. Shortly before the end of the 1914–18 war, the symphonic poem *Taras Bulba* came into being. Under the impact of his russo-philism—'since there are not in this world such fires and tortures as could break the strength of the Russian people'—he dedicated this work to the young Czech army. Next came the opera *Kátà Kabanová* (1919–1921), a free transcription of Ostrovsky's *Storm*, and a study of Old-Russian absolutism and despotism; then the *First String Quartet*, which was inspired by Tolstoy's novel *The Kreutzer Sonata*. At the end of his life, he was to put to music the sombre prison house scenes from Dostoievsky's *Memoirs from a House of the Dead* (1927–1928).[1]

The *feuilleton* section of the Brno daily paper *Lidové Noviny*, to which Janáček himself frequently contributed, brought to his notice two subjects for his most genuine and profound works— the opera *The Cunning Little Vixen* (1923) and the song-cycle *Diary of a Young Man who Vanished* (1919). In the children's corner of the same paper he found those charming children's rhymes which he was subsequently to set to music (1925). In composing those naïvely symbolical descriptions of animal life which Rudolf Těsnohlídek published in serial form, and in setting to music the passionate self-revelations of an anonymous peasant lad who fell prey to the enticement of a gypsy, Janáček's earth-bound pan-theism finds its full liberation. It encompasses the forest, the magic of the seasons and the hours of the day, the kinship between the human and animal worlds—above all, Eros, the elemental, inexorable, dominating law of life. '. . . And while writing this work, I was all the time thinking of you', he wrote to Kamilla Stoesslová referring to the *Diary of a Young Man who Vanished*. 'You, for me, were Zefka with the child in her arm, and he following her . . .'

[1] Cp. Chapter 14, pp. 184 ff., *Fairy-Tale* for Cello and piano. Other Russian themes which Janáček had intended to use were Tolstoy's *Anna Karenina* (1907) and *The Living Corpse*; he left sketches for both works.

Janáček's occasional contributions to the daily press dealt with the most varied questions of musical and cultural life. His ideas, propounded in a forceful, aphoristic language, contained many a truth, but also obvious errors—they were always, however, the quintessence of his very personal mode of thinking. His sentences seemed as if flung out by an intense perception wresting with expression. The verb is often missing; subject and attribute circumscribe, by way of sudden inspiration, an issue of fact for the presentation of which others might have needed several sentences. Janáček's is an impressionistic, and yet again expression-istic, style; compact, compressed, frequently sketchy; illumined, as it were, by a visionary sensuality and a highly original intellig-ence. In actual fact, Janáček's literary style was little more than the speech-motif technique of his music projected into words.

With his poetic-realistic perception and aphoristic-emotional mode of expression, Janáček inhabited the same artistic realm as the Silesian poet Petr Bezruč whose nationally and socially conscious didactic poetry was loved by the composer and in part set to music by him. *Kantor Halfar*, *Maryčka Magdonová* and *Seventy-thousand* reflect the social troubles and national suppres-sion, so familiar to Janáček and Bezruč, of the working population in the Eastern Moravian coal mining district. The dark, passionate tone of this and similar choral works of Janáček found in the Choral Society of Moravian Teachers under their conductor Ferdinand Vach a competent body of interpreters who were deeply devoted to the master's art.

In a letter to Bezruč (1 October, 1924), Janáček wrote: 'You are the only one whom I have not yet thanked for the kind thoughts expressed on the occasion of my seventieth birthday. I was gladdened by your lines: after all, you are the only one among my numerous artistic followers who has been able to peep into that little street, reverberating with music, where I am to be found. Some time ago, the two of us were standing next to each other, as it were, without knowing each other. I felt that I was very close to you, yet we did not meet. But your words found a great welcome within me, and they have called forth a torrent of sound, of rage, despair and pain. I heard the other day that the Swedes, Norwegians and the English simply devoured the chorus *Seventy-thousand*.'

On the 3rd of July 1924, Leoš Janáček reached his seventieth year. 'When I read in the paper today', he wrote to Max Brod in the winter of that year, 'that Suk's fiftieth and my seventieth birthday were to be celebrated—well, the day is not so far off—I walked out of the town into the snowy landscape, and in its peace I felt better.' Brno celebrated the event by the University's bestowal upon the master the honorary degree of Doctor of Philosophy (28 January 1925). With naïve pride Janáček henceforth attached the letters 'Dr.phil.' to his signature. Surprisingly, Prague took scant notice of the celebrations in honour of the Moravian composer. The National Theatre shrouded itself in silence; all they said was that a new production of a Janáček opera was unjustifiable on economic grounds since his works were not box-office draws. However, a number of concerts of Janáček's music were arranged such as the one put on by the local Society for New Music which included the *First String Quartet*, the *Violin Sonata*, the *Fairy-Tale* for cello and piano and some folk song arrangements.

Not even in his old age had Janáček succeeded entirely in dispelling some of the prejudices directed against him and his artistic convictions. One of the worst obstacles was his negative attitude towards Smetana, which had not been forgotten. Although in later years he revised his former position, and even studied the works of Smetana with thoroughness and occasional enthusiasm—this is born out by the very original glosses he wrote into the vocal scores of the older Master—yet he was still pursued by the memory of his former antipathy towards Smetana.

On the occasion of the centenary of Smetana's birth (1924), the Brno National Theatre invited Janáček to deliver a memorial address at the official celebration. The Master accepted, but the plan came to nothing since it was thought that Janáček might possibly give utterance to unorthodox views, deviating from the generally approved line on Smetana! This tactless treatment of a delicate occasion was a great disappointment to the old man.

In spite of Janáček's great general prestige, his position at home was still contested by certain circles, mainly in Prague. Abroad, however, his reputation and his fame were on the increase. His national stature had become so pre-eminent that he was now acclaimed by the world as a representative figure of international contemporary music.

CHAPTER 8

LAST YEARS

'I AM FILLED with the young spirit of our republic, with a young music. I do not belong to those who have stayed behind, but to those who would rather look forward. I know that we have grown, and I do not see this growing process in terms of pains, in reminiscences of subjection and suffering. Let us cast all this from us! Let us imagine that we have to look to the future. We are a people that must take their place in the world. We are the heart of Europe. And the beating of this heart should be audible to Europe.'

These words were spoken by Janáček in London, on the occasion of a reception during his visit of 1926. They are a characteristic avowal of his proud confidence and of the European-ism into which his nationalism had flowed. At the invitation of English friends, particularly the tireless champion of Czech music, Rosa Newmarch, Janáček had to come to London in the spring of 1926 where he was received with traditional British hospitality and generosity. The concert given on the 6th of May at Wigmore Hall, at which the *First String Quartet*, the *Violin Sonata*, the Wind Suite *Youth* and the *Fairy-Tale* for cello and piano were performed, was a great success. 'Incessant applause and calls for the composer, who was visibly moved, repeatedly thanking audience and performers from the platform.'[1] The

[1]From a report on Janáček's journey to England, *Hudební besídka*, 1926.

master had singled out for special praise the inspired interpretation of his *Violin Sonata* by Miss Adila Fachiri.[1] The reviews were without exception favourable; some of them placed the Moravian master on a level with Dvořák, designating him the successor to the latter in the appreciation of the English musical public. In the conductor Henry Wood, Janáček found a congenial interpreter (Wood was instrumental in bringing about a performance of the *Glagolitic Mass* in England) as well as a personal friend.

Germany, however, led the way among European countries in the early recognition of the significance of Janáček's work. Under the leadership of far seeing, modern minded musicians, a great number of German theatres mounted exemplary productions of Janáček's operas. This is what the composer said about the Berlin première of *Kátà Kabanová*[2] (under Fritz Zweig) in May, 1926: 'I had never realised that this piece was so good. I think I have heard this opera for the first time at this performance, and that I have understood it properly for the first time.' Hamburg, Cologne, Düsseldorf, Bremen, Essen, Munich, Karlsruhe, Kassel, Erfurt, Koenigsberg, Breslau—everywhere the same deep understanding for his music. At a chamber-music evening in Berlin (December, 1926), devoted exclusively to Janáček's works, the London programme with the addition of the *Concertino* was repeated with the greatest success.

Shortly after, at the invitation of the Berlin periodical *Die Literarische Welt*, Janáček took part in a symposium on the influence of Beethoven upon modern music. His reply, which excited much comment at the time, shall be quoted here in full: 'When I was twenty-five years of age, I already had Beethoven's *Missa Solemnis* at my fingertips. I conducted it in Brno on the 2nd of April, 1879. It is no use denying it: Beethoven's works have never

[1] In a letter of November 28th, 1926, Janáček stated that Miss Fachiri had 'breathed life into the long notes in the first movement so that they spoke of a soul tormented by restlessness.'

[2] On this occasion, Janáček made the acquaintance of Arnold Schönberg and Franz Schreker. Both composers were strongly impressed by *Kátà Kabanová*.

made me enthusiastic, never taken me out of myself. They have never transported me into the realm of ecstasy. I arrived at the bottom of them too soon. And quickly therefore, they have fallen to the bottom of my soul. In their broad sweep, I felt heavenly clouds; their power and the sun of their melodies illuminated every single cloud and dispelled every shadow. And over it all, the moon poured its yearning. But what is the good of it—I want to capture the clouds themselves, I want to sink my eye in the blue of the sky, I want to bundle the very sunrays in my fist, I want to plunge into the shadow, I want to cry myself into the core of yearning: all this in full immediacy. In the choir of the Leipzig Conservatoire I was placed among the first basses. Reinecke conducted Beethoven's *Missa Solemnis*—this, too, was towards the end of 1879. But I played truant; I missed the rehearsals and kept away from the performance of the work.'

These lines cast an interesting light upon the persistence of Janáček's judgment, upon the inflexible consequentiality of his mind, even when he was in the wrong. In view of these opinions, it is interesting to note that two years later, in a fulminating article, Janáček championed the preservation of the Bertramka, the well-known country-house in Prague where Mozart completed his *Don Giovanni*—according to Janáček the 'opera of all operas'.

At the age of seventy, the master had become a European, not to say an international figure. More and more often he was seen at the festivals of the *International Society of Contemporary Music*. His works were played at Salzburg (1923), Venice (1925) and Frankfurt (1927). To Frankfurt he even took a Czech peasant-band which, clad in its colourful national costumes, was to be seen and heard at an exhibition called 'Music in the life of the Nations'. At the International Music Festival in Prague (1925), *The Cunning Little Vixen* was given for the first time in the Czech capital under the direction of Otakar Ostrčil; 'but not the way I should have liked it' was, however, the composer's comment.

Janáček was fond of travelling abroad and stimulated by meeting the artists from all countries. In a *feuilleton* about the Music Festival at Venice he wrote: 'I like these festivals of modern music. There were twenty-eight composers, as many compositions, and none of them at all alike. The will to compose was more in evidence than real, explosive invention; yet the latter was more frequent than artistically rounded works. A lot of energy was wasted on comic music . . . Believe me, if you do not already know it, that music by itself cannot express love or hate, sadness or gaiety. Music can laugh, but her laughter cannot compel laughter. In music, there is neither merriment nor irony, neither satire nor humour nor joviality, neither burlesque nor persiflage, neither travesty nor masquerade. Yet, these days, people are longing for gay music.' Janáček's late maturity, his artistic wisdom, his realism that found its sublimation in a second classicism are expressed in these sentences.

However, the music which the master gave to the world in his old age was still 'young music'. In the year of his seventieth birthday, the wind-suite *Youth* came into being; a serenely contemplative reminiscence of his convent years at Old Brno, containing the high-spirited march of the blue-tits, as the pupils of the institute with their blue uniforms were called. The artistic experiences gained by Janáček on his visits to international festivals, however, helped to shape the sparkling instrumental style of the above work, as they inspired the conception of the *Concertino* for piano and chamber-orchestra (1925), the *Capriccio* (1926) for the one-armed pianist Otakar Hollmann, and above all, the worldly and brilliant *Sinfonietta* (1926). Janáček's late cosmopolitanism must surely have been responsible, too, for his choice of Karel Čapek's utopian play *The Makropulos Case* as the libretto for his opera of the same name (1925). While Čapek in his drama

Act I from the opera 'The Makropulos Case' from the performance in Düsseldorf, 1956

Photo : Jurgen Theis

*A scene from 'The Cunning Little Vixen' fro
the Felsenstein Production in Berlin, 1956*

Janáček in Venice, 1925 at the International Festival of Contemporary Music

The composer listening to the waves at Flushing, 1926

With Sir Henry Wood, 1926

dealt with the problem of physical immortality and its dreadful psychological and social consequences, Janáček gave profundity to the action by a new motive—the heroine's yearning for redemption from her hopeless semi-eternal existence, and the compassion for her aroused in us. *The Makropulos Case* is Janáček's only operatic subject lacking in any national or popular tendencies, and the style of this work approaches most closely to the international idiom current in the nineteen-twenties.

The resplendent *Sinfonietta*, on the other hand, is imbued with national feeling. It begins and ends with the festive fanfares of trumpets, trombones and kettledrums; a sound-combination which Janáček had treasured since the days of his boyhood when he took part as a chorister in the celebration of High Mass at Rychaltice, which he was particularly fond of recalling during his last years (cp. the *Glagolitic Mass*). In composing the *Sinfonietta*, he had in mind the 'free Czech man of today, the beauty and joyfulness of his soul, but also his strength and his resolution to fight and win through'. Thus, this work, too, was dedicated to the armed forces of Czechoslovakia.

The national idea increasingly gained in sublimity with Janáček, and when, in 1926, he set to music the Old Slavonic version of the Mass from the time of St. Cyril and St. Method, he approached this complex task with his thoughts on the millennium, occurring in 1929, of St. Wenceslaus, the patron saint of Bohemia; a millennium which had its topical counterpart in the tenth anniversary of the foundation of the Czech state (1928). 'I intended in this work to enshrine my faith in the security of the nation; not on a religious basis, but on the fundament of a morality and vigour which calls upon God as its witness.'[1] At the age of seventy-two, he produced in the *Glagolitic Mass* a work of well-nigh indomitable vitality, a work which, by virtue of its racial and artistic aims, comes close to Stravinsky's *Sacre du*

[1]From an interview in *Literarní svět* (The Literary World), 1928.

Printemps. Janáček had to defend himself against the view exemplified by a critic who called him 'a credulous dotard'; but then, the Mass, in more than one respect, broke with the traditions of Catholic church music. Never before had a musician dared to take up before God the self-assured, confident position of Janáček, who here encounters his Creator as a being on equal terms. It is the master's pantheism, experienced to its extreme limits, which here triumphantly confirms in him the feeling of being of a nature kindred to, nay, of the very essence, of the Creator.

'Never before has my head been so empty as now after the *Makropulos Case*, the *Glagolitic Mass*, the *Capriccio* and the *Nursery Rhymes* (*Říkadla*). Usually, one work immediately follows another. Now I wish that I might find some uncomposed libretto; something unrestricted, untrammelled, something out of another world—in short, I am not quite sure yet myself: if possible something that is rooted in the earth, or in a spiritual sphere ...'

In these words, which were directed to Max Brod, Janáček betrays the unrest which in his last years usually took hold of him after the completion of a major work. On another occasion, he told me that he always became sad on concluding a composition, for 'the book of life closed itself, too'. His creative power feared the void, and the secret of his creative vitality lay in evading it.

Of Dostoievsky's *Memoirs from a House of the Dead*, and in particular, of Janáček's adaptation of these shattering confessions of human misery, it may truly be said that they are 'rooted in the earth', and at the same time, extend upwards to a 'spiritual sphere'. It was, in particular, the element of Christian redemption inherent in Dostoyevsky's conception, which prompted Janáček to dramatise and form into a libretto some of these reports, although, to be sure they are wanting in action. Yet the static, narrative, construction of Dostoievsky's *Memoirs* was not wholly suited to Janáček's aims; he therefore freely refashioned the original, thus creating a series of dynamically intensified scenes which, in their humanity and metaphysical import, are among the highest flights of his creativeness. Janáček's personal warm-heartedness was sublimated here into Christian optimism; a message of deliverance which places the Moravian master among the august company of the great Slav moralists Tolstoy and Dostoievsky; a further link with the latter is the psychological penetration which Janáček shared with him.

In his last works,[1] Janáček has once more revealed the full depth and range of his humanity. The *Second String Quartet* (1928), too, belongs to the compositions of his late and, as it were, second classicism; a clear, serene style in which emotion and structure are in perfect equilibrium, in which forms have crystallised into well proportioned conciseness, movements are being linked by thematic and structural evolution, and the folkloristic elements appear artistically refined.

In a very personal, confessional letter to Max Brod, of the 18th of January, 1928, Janáček lifts the veil from the innermost source of the inspiration of his old age. In it he says: '. . . You know that my motifs grow from the earth, from animals and humans—that they are united with everything that exists. It's only the keyboard they fight shy of. The vision of my operatic figures will always live in reality . . . Tell me, should it be possible for me to own publicly who the being is in whom my motifs become crystallised?[2] Has any writer ever betrayed this? With a painter, it is no secret. But with a composer? Would people take it amiss if he publicly revealed the allegiances of his soul, the bonds of his art? For thirteen years now, my soul has upheld loyalty, and it has never deviated from the path of a simple friendly relationship. This sounds incredible, but it is so. Can

[1] A suggestion, cautiously received by Janáček, of writing the stage music for Gerhard Hauptmann's *Schluck and Jau*, resulted in four extant numbers. Janáček was busy with this project in the spring of 1928.

[2] The allusion is to an essay in which Janáček discussed the origin of his musical motifs.

anyone undo this? Can perhaps my wife sever this bond?[1] I am fully aware of the psychological significance underlying this attachment of my motifs to reality. The intelligibility of the motifs is enhanced, their impact and immediacy are heightened. This is quite manifest in my works. I have grown up with this manner of working—and have outgrown it . . .'

Janáček has here described his relationship with Kamilla Stoesslová as an artistically inspiring bond, and as a source of energy for his creativeness. The four movements of the *Second String Quartet* are imbued with the happiness of this love. They are intimate monologues, reflections of a mature and fully conscious passion, by no means a 'sunset glow', but the climax of his creative and emotional life. Written in twenty-two days, this quartet became the proud manifesto of the composer's love for Kamilla Stoesslová.

At the time of Janáček's seventieth birthday, a decisive change occurred in his relationship to his friend. In view of his temperament, it was unavoidable that his feelings, which in former years had been so heartwarming and stimulating, should now be transformed into an all-demanding passion. 'I have begun to write something beautiful', he told Kamilla on the 1st of February, 1928. 'Our life will be contained in it. I shall call it love letters. I think it will sound marvellous. How many treasured experiences we have had together! Like little flames, these will light up in my soul and become the most beautiful melodies. Imagine it! The first piece I have written in memory of Hukvaldy. My impression when I saw you for the first time! Now I am working on the second movement; I think our summer at Luhačovice will rise up in that . . . The whole work will be kept together by a special instrument. It is called viola d'amour—the viola of love. How I am looking forward to it! In this work, I shall be alone

[1] Zdenka Janáček had suffered much under the relationship of her husband and Mme. Stoesslová. After Janáček's death, she had to go to court in order to annul a clause in the composer's will which instituted Mme. Stoesslová as sole beneficiary.

with you. No third person besides us . . .'

The greater the fulfilment life granted him, the more he loved the earth and its gifts. Death he did not fear—elemental natures of Janáček's kind are always familiar with it; but he sought to avoid death, to keep away from it as long as possible. At times, and more frequently so as he grew older, intimations of death invaded, like an icy chill, the late-summer glow of his vitality. All the more urgently he then sought the friendship and womanliness of Kamilla. His unexpected end during a happy summer-vacation at Hukvaldy seemed the act of a kind providence. On an excursion into the woods, one of Kamilla's children had lost his way. Janáček went to look for the missing boy. Tired and heated by some hours of strenuous walking, he took a rest in the open. Already the next day, the first signs of pneumonia appeared. The master was taken into the hospital at Moravská Ostrava, and there he passed away peacefully. It was on the 12th of August, 1928, shortly after the completion of his seventy-fourth year. His body was laid out in a side-chapel of the Old Brno Abbey Church, where he had begun his musical career. The official funeral procession, however, set out from the Brno National Theatre, where the consecration had taken place.

This home-coming is symbolic. Hukvaldy, the starting-point of his life, was to be its last station. Between these poles, there is the vault of his career, which, firmly rooted in nature and the people, carried his work far and wide over the globe. Yet he remained the son of his native soil. After the eruptive phase of his youth, this fiery nationalist, this revolutionary and dramatist had, at the end of his life risen to the sphere of pure humanity, of timelessness and objectivity. In his appearance as well as in his development, Janáček reminds us of the old Verdi. As, in the last operas of the Italian master, style and expression are trans-figured and expanded to embrace a benign, understanding humanity; like Verdi's, his religion, unorthodox but of profound ethical strength determined his life-philosophy; like Verdi he returned, after world-wide triumphs, to the rustic homestead (which, in a sense, he had never abandoned); Hukvaldy and St. Agata were more than the last stations of two lives—they were the symbols of fulfilment, the return to the origin, to the people, to earth and God.

To Janáček's friends and pupils and to the musical world, the master's sudden death was a great blow, the more severe as it fell so unexpectedly. If ever life is transcended by death as by its organic-mystical fulfilment—an overflowing of life which gives existence its ultimate meaning—then this was the true fate of the dionysian child of nature, Leoš Janáček. In *The Cunning Little Vixen* he had given expression to this allegory. Perhaps the finest distinction of his genius lay in his capacity for making the response of a visionary to the mystery of life.

II

JANÁČEK'S WORK

CHAPTER 9

THE FOLKLORISTIC ROOTS OF JANÁČEK'S MUSIC

'FOLK SONG—I have lived in it since childhood. In folk song the entire man is enshrined, his body and soul, his milieu—everything. He who is rooted in folk song, becomes a complete man. Folk song expresses the spirit of the pure individual and his God-given culture, barring all secondary and fortuitous elements. Therefore I believe that as soon as our art-music originates from this popular source, we shall all become brethren in the creations of that music; a community will thus arise, encompassing all mankind. Folk song unites a people; it unites nations and mankind itself in one spirit of happiness and contentment.[1]

Janáček, as we have seen, derived his personal and artistic culture from his profound affinity with the soul of the people. A warm-hearted, socially-minded man, strongly rooted in Nature, he consistently retained in his music a continuous link with his native folk music. It was the perpetual source of his inspiration, the vitalising agency from which sprang his declamatory realism, his characteristic melody, and his individual harmony and rhythm. And it was this source which, at a time when European music inclined to a cosmopolitan eclecticism, saved him from the clichés of this eclecticism and from the perfervid extremes of the post-impressionist period.

[1]From a speech by Janáček in London after a Concert of some of his choruses, 1926.

Already, as a young man, Janáček had begun to collect and set the folk songs of his native country. His analytical method of classification raises his activity in the realm of folk song to the rank of a modern scientific investigation, and this at a time when, under the influence of romanticism, folk song was set in stereo-typed, classical moulds, and was regarded as scarcely more than a picturesque or sentimental curiosity. Almost twenty years before Bartok, Janáček had drawn attention to the rhythmic variety, the modality, and frequent exotic and archaic tonalities, the unorthodox harmonies and modulations, and last but not least, to the strange magic that runs through the accompaniments of these Eastern Moravian and Slovak[1] melodies, by bagpipes, dulcimer (czimbalon) and other instruments. Our understanding of the characteristics of Janáček's idiom must arise from its affinities with the folk music of the eastern parts of Moravia and Silesia, altogether with that of the Slavonic East.

Nowhere within the Slavonic group of peoples perhaps is there to be found as markedly dual a cultural orientation towards East and West as with the Czechoslovakians. This is, in the main, conditioned by the geographical situation of the country, whose most important province, Bohemia, has maintained close relations with Europe and the West in general, whereas the southern and eastern provinces—the eastern parts of Moravia and Slovakia—gravitate towards the East. This contrast which, as I have shown in a previous context, is partly based on historical and psychological factors, has at all times determined the character of Czech culture, quite apart from the political antagonism between the industrialised and urbanised Bohemia and the mainly agrarian, conservative and feudal Slovakia. In the music of Czechoslovakia, this contrast is characterised by the classic-

[1]The Eastern Moravian province, i.e. the territory east of the river Morava is often referred to as *Slovácko*, a name not identical with *Slovensko* which stands for *Slovakia*, the arc-shaped eastern half of Czechoslovakia. Janáček's musical idiom can be specifically compared with the idiom of the *Slovácko*-district to which the composer's home district, the *Lachian* and *Valachian* region (Lašsko and Valašsko) belong.

romantic orientation of Smetana and Dvořák on the one hand, and the realistic, eastern folklorism of Janáček on the other.

The Morava (March), the chief river of Moravia, is usually considered the dividing line between these two spheres of Czech culture. Accordingly, the character of the folk music in the two halves of the country is of a distinctly individual cast.

Historical investigations have stressed the close relationship between the folk songs and dances of Bohemia and the western part of Moravia with the melodies and structural types of the Seventeenth and Eighteenth century European music. The material that was extant in medieval traditions became assimilated during the period of baroque and early classical music. The instrumental and dance character (common chord motifs) of the melodies is unmistakable; diatonicism predominates in the harmony, and the formal structure shows the customary symmetrical periodisations into four and eight-bar groups. This was the basis for the musical idiom of the Bohemian craftsman musicians of the Eighteenth century (the Mannheim composers above all) and the Nineteenth century, including Smetana and Dvořák (notwithstanding the latter's strongly panslavistic tendencies). The style of these musicians strongly professed the allegiance of Bohemia, and indeed of the Czechoslovakian West, to the world of the European West.

In the eastern half, however, we encounter a live continuity of popular traditions, which has hardly been subjected to change in the course of centuries. The land-bound country folk have stubbornly opposed the urban influences of the Eighteenth and Nineteenth centuries; thus, their language, their music, their visual arts, and above all, their abundant crafts remained untouched by the dissipation of modern life.

In contradistinction to the folk music of Bohemia, the songs and dances of Eastern Moravia and Slovakia have originated in the vocal sphere. Here, dance and song are one, there is singing during the dancing, and words and tunes emerge from age-old traditions. A precise differentiation of the two types is hardly feasible. The structure of the eastern folksongs, with their irregular rhythms, their free periodisation and frequent modality, indicates the great age of these melodies; it also proves their dependence on the laws of language.

Janáček's melodic idiom, too, grew out of the language. Out of short, frequently abrupt melodic fragments, he constructed his lyrical arcs and dramatic passages with their numerous changes of time, their bizarre interval steps, free form and strong leaning towards modality. The origin of his melody from the prosody of language, i.e. from primarily vocal roots, is unmistakable, and can frequently also be traced in his instrumental music, as we shall see in due course. This fact accounts for the predominance of vocal compositions (operas and choral works) as compared with instrumental works in Janáček's *oeuvre*.[1]

In the relation of the composer Janáček to folk music, three characteristic aspects can perhaps be established: the collection and setting of folk songs and their occasional employment, mainly in certain early works (the *Lachian Dances*, the ballet *Rákocz Rákoczy*, the opera *Beginning of a Romance*, *Folk Songs from Hukvaldy*, the *Silesian Songs*, etc.); the adoption of folk song and its fully personal stylisation and intensivation, amounting to what is in fact a re-creation (*Jenufa*, *The Cunning Little Vixen*, the *Diary of a Young Man who Vanished*); lastly, the sublimation of the folk-idiom into the large-spaced linearity of his late works (the wind-sextet *Youth*, the *Sinfonietta*, the *Glagolitic Mass*, the *Second String Quartet*).

In the early male choruses, Janáček's inclination towards free rhythmical structures in the manner of Eastern Moravian or Slovakian folk songs is already apparent. Adapting himself

[1] cp: Max Brod, *Sternenhimmel*, p. 26: 'Janáček's word-melodies sound virtually like abbreviated, now compressed, now expanded Moravian-Slovakian folk songs.'

closely to the frequently irregular syllable-number of his texts, Janáček changes his metre, if need be, in every bar, as, for instance, in the chorus: *Inconstant Love* (*Nestálost lásky*). In this we find a succession of 8/8, 7/8, 8/8, 6/8, 9/8, etc. At the same time, he renounces customary time-signatures, as for instance, in the chorus *True Love* (*Láska opravdivá*), or *You Cannot Escape Your Destiny* (*Osudu neujdeš*).

This manner of setting texts to music is undoubtedly influenced from the sphere of folk song. In contrast to the conventional type of folk song setting with its approximation to uniform rhythmic pattern, Janáček provides a sensitive musical portrayal of the verbal metre with its natural accentuation and its fluctuations of expression. Thus, in his settings of folk song texts, sometimes the tempo indications, too, change from bar to bar (*You Cannot Escape Your Destiny*). This realism, as we see, corresponds to the acute aural sensitivity with which Janáček closely allays the psychological elements of poetic mood and atmosphere to the rhythmic-melodic element.

Significant for Janáček's manner of vitalising, and, as it were, re-creating a given folk melody, is the choral song, 'It is a long, long way'. ('Daleko, široko') from *Jenufa*. The melody shows interesting points of contact with an Eastern Moravian folk song.[1]

Example 1

Janáček must have known this song well, for he was to use its text again in a choral song of his own composition which is

[1] The music examples Nos. 1, 2, 3, 5, 6, 11 used in this chapter are reprinted with the kind permission of the Editor of *The Musical Quarterly*, New York. Compare the author's study 'The Music of Leoš Janáček—Its origin in Folklore', *The Musical Quarterly*, Vol. XLI, No. 2.

almost identical with the *Jenufa* chorus. His version shows a certain likeness with the folk melody, e.g. the mirror inversion of the rhythm ♪♪♪|♪♪♩ which is typical of the Slovakian folk music; there are, however, definite divergences, such as the different placing of the melodic climax, and, generally, Janáček's simplified periodisation.

Example 2

There is, to be sure, another and simpler version of this folk-song, whose final melodic phrase shows an interesting agreement with the closing cadence of the *Jenufa*-chorus.

Example 3

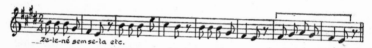

In the *Diary of a Young Man who Vanished* such transformations of folk song types are specially frequent, whereby Janáček modally inflects a diatonic folk song form, thus enriching the melodic expressiveness and harmonic colouring of the composition.

Example 4

4a. *Folk Song from Eastern Moravia*, Už tebe, Anička . . .

4b. *Diary of a Young Man Who Vanished*, No. XIV.

The frequent occurrence of modality in Janáček's music can be traced back to various influences, among which his training in church music is certainly of importance. In the main, however, Janáček's modal leanings have their origin in the Eastern Moravian and Slovakian folk music, which, in its turn, has been influenced by the music of the Slavonic East, and especially by Russian folk and church music.[1]

The preference for modal colours in his melodic and harmonic conceptions was deeply rooted in Janáček's artistic personality. During his studies in Leipzig and Vienna, he had already invented modal melodies; the stubbornness with which he insisted, in disagreement with his Leipzig teacher, Grill, on the modal F as against the diatonic F sharp, in an exercise piece in G minor, is very revealing.[2]

Subsequently, Janáček put his modal style on a theoretical basis by saying that melodies without leading notes keep the tonality fluid and that above anything else, the expressive power of a melody is enhanced when the emphatic step from leading note to tonic is omitted. Whoever has appreciated the character of Janáček's melodies, will not easily forget their strong, dark, exotic beauty. In them live the melancholy minor mood, the rhapsodic rubato and the passionate exaltation of Eastern Slavonic folk music.

The lydian (augmented) fourth is one of the modal intervals most often found in folk music as also in Janáček; but dorian, phrygian, mixolydian, and aeolian modes are also encountered frequently. The charming dancing-song of the young foxes from *The Cunning Little Vixen*, for instance, derives its peculiar attractiveness from the pointed restatement of the lydian E.

[1]cp. Ch. 10, p. 111-113.
[2]Letter to Zdenka Schulz, Leipzig, 20 October 1879.

Example 5

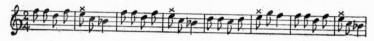

Similar melodies from folk music could be quoted in great number, such as the following little song in similar rhythm and partly lydian modality: *Folk Song from Strážnice*. Dycky sem ti říkával.

Example 6

Often, however, the modal quality of Janáček's melodies cannot be defined unequivocally. There are instances in which a modal character predominates, while the mode as such is not clearly indicated (e.g. *Taras Bulba*, opening subject, first part). Janáček frequently creates melodies on an apparently unorthodox tonal (not, however, atonal) basis; successions of notes which, as in certain Eastern Slavonic folk songs, are based on free, exotic scales. Recent researches (especially the publications of the Slovak musicologist Th. Hirner) have shown that the modal and quasi-modal tonalities of Slavonic folk music do not go back to Gregorian chant but are explained by the scale-wise organisation of the harmonics of certain shepherds' flutes, such as the mixolydian Fujura from the Detva district in Slovakia.

Free treatment of modality exists also in those cases where the beginning and end of a melody are in different keys. One of the most beautiful examples of this kind is the chorus 'Every couple must bide its time of suffering' from *Jenufa*. The marvellous melodic line begins in dorian A flat and ebbs away in phrygian A flat.

Example 7

Nor are such cases rare in folk music: *Folk Song from Hukvaldy.*
"Proč Kalinko . . ."

Example 8

The vocal character of Janáček's melodies too, points in many
ways to the sphere of folk-music. Of special interest are the
numerous passages in his works where he transplants vocal types
of melody into the instrumental sphere. The following little
dance song from Velká in Moravia is a specimen of a type which
Janáček has restated in instrumental terms more than once.[1]

Example 9

9 (a) *Folksong from Velká.* "Byla jedna . . ."

9 (b) *Sinfonietta, 2nd movement.*

Also the lively dance-theme of the fourth movement of the
Sinfonietta is a good example of those melodies of Janáček
constructed from short two- or three-bar phrases.

[1] A variant of the same kind appears also in the fourth movement of the Concertino.

Example 10

The theme is varied, in the manner of an ostinato, by changes in the scoring and key; it is enlivened by attractive countervoices whose freshness of figuration reminds one of similar improvisations undertaken by instruments accompanying a folk melody. But let us compare the *Sinfonietta* theme with the following vocal melody from the district of Hustopeče:

Example 11

The relationship of the two melodies is unmistakable. In folk song, to be sure, we find that rhythmic accents are frequently paraphrased by free rubato-metres; a feature we encounter again and again in Janáček's music, too. This peculiarity often gives rise to polyrhythmic structures, especially if the free-metre paraphrases occur above a repeated and constant rhythm.

Example 12. The Cunning Little Vixen, p. 10.

Attention should be drawn here to another frequently met melodic formula since it is based on a characteristic interval

pattern of Moravian folk music—the stereotyped motif that
results from the combination of a second with its adjoining third
or fourth, or its inversion.

Example 13

(a) Folk song from Detva.
(b) Folk song from Eastern Moravia.
(c) Folk song from Eastern Moravia.

A typical vocal melisma,[1] this pattern seems to be ever-present
in Janáček's subconsciousness, frequently operating as a germ of
melodic formation.

Example 14. Diary of a Young Man who Vanished:
   (a) No. XVII. (b) No. XIX. (c) No. XXII. (d) First String
Quartet, 1st Movement.

[1]In its origin probably an ancient intonation formula it is still preserved in many regions
of European folk music.

The Kyrie of the *Glagolitic Mass* is developed from such a motif played by the cellos:

Example 15

In the Gloria it appears in this transformation:

Example 16

In the Credo it assumes this shape:

Example 17

The counter-melody of the ostinato theme of the organ solo at the end of the mass shows the following form:

Example 18

But how much tauter and deeper in expression does this sequence of notes appear in the above examples of the Kyrie and Credo; how clearly and sharply delineated it is here, owing to the verbal accentuation and the religious pathos of the text.

These examples strike us as so many transformations of the already-quoted folk songs (viz. Ex. 13).

A feature of special interest are the instrumental accompaniments in Eastern Moravian and Slovakian folk music, that also occur in Janáček's compositions. The extent to which he absorbed the technique and the aesthetic character of popular instruments is apparent in the wayward accompaniment patterns of his melodies. It is frequently the characteristic sound and technical range of bagpipes and dulcimer (czimbalons) which provide the basis of Janáček's bass-parts. Pedal-like basses; harp-like chord arpeggios; arabesques which, as it were, rotate around a principal note; motifs formed by the agglomeration of short notes—all these are born from the spirit of the age-old instruments of folk singers and village musicians; a race that seems to live in Janáček himself. Such motifs, in their elemental primitiveness and sensuousness of sound, underline the harmonic character of a melody and often invest it with a specific emotion.

Janáček loved those timbres, and, in particular, he never tired of varying unceasingly the vibrant, rhapsodic tone of the dulcimer (cp. the *Diary of a Young Man who Vanished*, Nos. 10, 13, 16, etc.). In the second part of the opera *The Excursions of Mr. Brouček*, he has used the bagpipes as an accompaniment to the

Hussite chorale 'Ye, who are the warriors of God'. He once wrote to a friend:[1] '. . . I value the bagpipe for the mellowness and pensive quality of its tone; it carries into the modern orchestra a noble, pensive sound, which is yet more soulful than that of the organ.' Many of his melodies have the character of a bagpipe tune, such as the song from *The Cunning Little Vixen* (Ex. 5) quoted above.

'My last creative period, I feel, is like a new burgeoning of my soul. I have settled my affairs with the world and am trying to come quite close to the heart of humble Czech folk.'[2] Janáček himself reckons this last creative period from his seventieth year.

The melodic character of his late works shows a certain tranquillity and introspection. In the wind sextet *Youth* (*Mládí*, 1924) he strives for the thematic unity of the single movements, so too, in the *First String Quartet* (1923), and in the *Second String Quartet* (1928) there is to be found a melodic relationship between the opening theme of the first movement and the wonderful love chant of the third movement, as well as some sections of the finale. The spirit of folk music appears here transfigured, and its profound humanity sublimated. The opening theme of the *Second String Quartet* (*Intimate Letters*) is given its air of ardent reverie by its 'popular' sixths and the free rubato rhythm.

Example 19

[1] From a letter to Č. Žíbrt, 1918.
[2] Saying of Janáček from the last years of his life.

The best melodic ideas in Janáček's late works are distinguished by expansive lines and lyrical pathos; see the following passage from *The House of the Dead: Skuratov's theme*, p. 74.

Example 20

He often employs the basic formulae of popular melody types, constructing extensive passages of a movement from this material in ostinato form, as for instance in the 'Gloria' of the *Glagolitic Mass* (viz. Ex. 16).

Towards the end of his life, Janáček carried his experience of folk music to the extreme limits of simplification, spiritualisation, and humanisation.

CHAPTER 10

THE STYLE OF JANÁČEK'S MUSIC

JANÁČEK'S musical style was in the closest possible rapport with his affinity to folk song, with his personality and temperament. His musical idiom was the direct expression of his inner life—one might almost say that in his case there was an absence of that intermediary stage of sublimation, existing in most artists, in which the primary creative impulse is transformed into the formed artistic idea. His music represents one of those rare cases in the history of the arts where an unbroken continuity between the man and the artist engenders a valid life-work which, notwithstanding its spontaneity and naturalness, is not lacking in intellectual stylisation and spiritual significance. In order to find analogies, one must revert to such men as Haydn and Verdi, relatively uncomplicated in their psychology; their artistic expression is, as with Janáček, a direct projection of their personal conduct and approach to life.

Since the publication of *Jenufa*, the discussion of the problems involved in Janáček's musical style has not ceased. The apparent formlessness of his ideas, the sparseness of his technical realisation, the primitive shape of his formal devices, the many apparent illogicalities of his harmonic progressions, the manifest mistakes and miscalculations of the scoring—all these are continually preferred as arguments against Janáček's art. It would be pointless to deny these peculiarities in Janáček's style; they are among the stark facts of his musical idiom, and for the experienced, yet unbiassed listener, these imperfections—judgment on which must be conditional at best—prove to be strong points rather than weaknesses of his style.

Janáček's work has been divided into four periods: the years of his youth, to which belong his student's efforts in Prague, Leipzig, and Vienna, written under influences of classic and romantic models; his renunciation of classicism and the creation of his personal idiom, rooted in folk song and speech-inflection (the oratorio *Amarus*, *Fairy-Tale* for Cello and Piano, *Jenufa*); the extension of this style by means of assimilating elements of contemporary European music (the *First String Quartet*, the *Diary of a Young Man who Vanished*, the *Concertino*, the *Capriccio*, the operas of his middle period); and finally his last years—Janáček's second classicism, as it were—to which belong his late works (the Wind Sextet *Youth*, the *Sinfonietta*, *The House of the Dead*, the *Glagolitic Mass*, the *Second String Quartet*).

The four creative periods reflect, by and large, the evolution of Janáček's musical thought. They mirror the transformations in, and to a certain extent the quality of, his human experience, which in the works of his old age was to be illumined by a new radiant lyricism. Above all, they correspond to the phases, discussed in the preceding chapter, of his relation to folk music.

Only a small portion of the works of Janáček's youth has remained extant. Most compositions of his student years in Leipzig and Vienna he subsequently destroyed. The trend of his early musical thought clearly emerges, however, from existing exercise books and from later works of this period. Seeking for a personal style, Janáček within the frame of classical formalism employs idioms of contemporary late-romantic music. It was Mendelssohn, Schumann, Wagner, Rubinstein—chiefly, however, Dvořák—who supplied the foundation of his early musical grammar. But even in those days, Janáček instinctively followed a definite trend—his eclecticism was by no means indiscriminate —and the composer whose influence became gradually more decisive for his style, was Antonín Dvořák. It is due to the impact of Dvořák that Janáček, as Vladimír Helfert has noted,[1] found his personal idiom. In the *Suite* for String Orchestra, the *Idyll* for String Orchestra, and in the *Lachian Dances*, to be sure, Janáček has, in places, approached Dvořák's model so closely that one cannot help thinking that his highest aim was to copy the older composer as slavishly as possible. There are other moments, however, where an individual manner emerges from the accents of Dvořák; where Janáček's fascination with the model seems to liberate some personal vision and unsuspected creative powers, as in this example from the third movement of the *Idyll* for String Orchestra:

Example 21

This melodic widening and stretching of an interval is one of the typical devices of Janáček's art. In the works of his maturity, too, emotional climaxes are often brought about by this effect,

[1] Vladimír Helfert, *Leoš Janáček*, p. 346.

as for instance the expression of loving compassion in the closing
refrain of the male chorus *Maryčka Magdonová* (1906).

Example 22

How lasting the influence of Dvořák was on the work of
Janáček, is proven, for example, by the main theme of the
symphonic ballad *The Fiddler's Child* (1912). In the one-movement
form of this symphonic poem, as well as in the melody of the
musician, the allegiance to Dvořák is quite obvious.

Example 23

Janáček's middle period is characterised by his folkloristic
interests and the absorption of speech-inflection into his melodic-
rhythmic invention. The development of melodic technique
out of speech-inflection is nothing new in itself. The Russians,
Puccini, Wagner, Debussy, and Monteverdi have developed their
melodic style largely from the declamation of language. The
novelty of Janáček's approach, however, lies in his realisation of
the melodic element (besides the rhythmic) of human speech;
in the elaboration of the speech-melos, reflecting the shades of
human emotions. The swelling and fading, rising and falling in
the tone of speech, the fluctuations of rhythm, the timbre and

colour of all these revealed to him psychological facets which he untiringly registered with a well-nigh scientific thoroughness. The principle of declamatory truthfulness already developed to an admirable degree of precision by Janáček's predecessors, is further enriched and enhanced by its union with the melodic element. The fundamental impulse of Janáček's melodic invention rises from his strong affinity to nature and earth. He professes: '. . . I listen to the midge, the fly, to the owl's sad lay . . . My register of human speech-melodies grows. I marvel at the thousandfold phenomena of rhythm in the world of light, colour, and forms, and my music grows young in the eternal rhythmic youth of Nature.' And again: 'I listen stealthily to the conversation of passers-by, watching their facial expression, noting the environment of the speaker, the company present, the time, light, dusk, coldness, and warmth. I find the reflection of all this in the written melody. How many variations I have encountered here in the speech-melody of one and the same word! Here it was radiant and flexible, there hard and piercing.'[1]

From such raw material is Janáček's music fashioned. The ruggedness of his invention is ennobled by its truth, which is absolute and a token of pure humanity. The fleeting impression of a sound or rhythm becomes a musical formula; a few notes crystallise into a motif—concise, dramatic, full of emotion— a significant gesture, a symbol of humanness. 'Model sketching of a musician' is what Janáček called his method. But he was not always satisfied with the bare outline. His melodies possess fine articulation, an interesting rhythmic structure, and are fascinating in the intensity of their expression and tonal and harmonic colouring.

Janáček has often developed entire scenes and instrumental movements from such musical micro-organisms. The emphatic Adagio close, with its rising Tenth, in Jenufa's first scene 'O

[1]Max Brod, Leoš Janáček, p. 28.

mother Mary' (p. 8) becomes the orchestral main motif (p. 150) later when Jenufa, as in the first scene, is wishing for the return of her faithless lover.

Example 24

This is one of many cases where Janáček operates with a kind of 'motif of recollection'. In *The Cunning Little Vixen* he develops the 61-bar long prelude to the second act as well as the orchestral accompaniment of the first scene in this act (p. 51-58) from a short melisma of the vixen, her innocently surprised exclamation at the sight of the badger's den. This motif in fact is to become one of the leading melodic characters of the opera. (cp. Ch. 11, p. 144).

Example 25

In *Kátà Kabanová*, the motif of the evil Kabanicha (p. 28) with its vehement rising Seventh, corresponds with her vocal phrase 'Thou shouldst have been silent . . .' (p. 30). This motif underlies an extensive part of the scene with her son Tichon (p. 28-33). One of the most beautiful lyrical examples of this kind is the closing scene of *Jenufa* (244) where the demi-semi-

quaver motif that dominates the scene, grows out of the first
words of the love-duet 'Now You See'.

Example 26

The pregnant, often acutely pointed interval-steps of Janáček's
melodies betray their origin in the sphere of the speech-motifs.
We often find diminished or augmented intervals; auxiliary
notes rotating around a principal note are just as characteristic
as the wide, explosive melodic leaps employed in depicting
strong effects. The comparison with Moussorgsky, and Russian
models in general, presents itself here. But whereas Moussorgsky's
realism tends towards unstylised naturalism, Janáček's melodic
phrases are, for the greater part, lyrically rounded, singable, and
emotionalised.[1]

A good example of Janáček's manner of transmuting a phrase
of speech-melody into a symmetrically built lyrical period is
found in the second scene of the first act of *Kátà Kabanová*
(57-58). The structural climax coincides here with the emotional
climax. Kátà tries with all means at her disposal to dissuade her
husband Tichon from setting out on his journey. The passage
begins with a variation on the lyrical Kátà-theme (p. 27); but
its continuation is shaped like a song ('If thou stayest behind, or
takest me with thee, I should love thee dearly . . .'). The rhythm
shows the characteristic mirror-inversion of Eastern Slavonic folk

[1] cp. Janáček's dictum: Moussorgsky has changed over from the Wagnerian motif to
those of language, without recognising the latter's beauty. If he had recognised it, he
would have dwelt with it.'

music; in the fifth bar of the Moderato section, however, the melodic line rises sharply, culminating on G sharp entering on a weak beat—a subtle nuance of lyrical emphasis.

Example 27

Ach, mein Täub-chen, wenn du da-heim blie-best o-der mich mit --- näh-mest, und ich dich so lieb ha-ben, herz -------------in-nig lieb ha-ben.

The influence of Moussorgsky, and of Russian music in general, has been of fundamental importance in Janáček's *oeuvre*.[1] As he orientated himself culturally and politically towards the Slavonic East, and in particular towards Russia, the great Slav mother-country, his music became consciously and unconsciously closer to the style of Russian national nineteenth-century music (Moussorgsky, Borodin, Tchaikovsky, Rubinstein) and of Russian folk and church music than to any other comparable Western zone of influence. This is shown, for instance, in the piano pieces *On an Overgrown Path* (1902-08) whose abrupt melodic design,

[1]The similarity of Moussorgsky's and Janáček's endeavours becomes apparent in a passage from a letter of the Russian composer, of 1876, where he says: 'I studied human speech; this made me realise the melody of language, and I arrived at a melodic form of recitative. This is what I should call a validly motivated melody . . .' *Truth* of artistic expression became the highest law for both masters; *beauty* had to subordinate itself to *truth*.

weighty chord and octave effects, ostinato-like accompaniments and overall impressionistic manner clearly point to Moussorgsky's *Pictures of an Exhibition.*

Example 28[1]

(a) Janáček: On an Overgrown Path: The little owl continues screeching.

(b) Moussorgsky: Pictures of an Exhibition: La cabane sur les pattes de poule.

[1] cp. Moussorgsky's *Samuel Goldberg and Schmuyle* and Janáček's *The Word Fails.*

Of the numerous passages in Janáček's music that can be traced back to Russian models, a few may be quoted. The wedding chorus from *Jenufa* ('Ah, mother, dear mother . . .', p. 208) for instance, with the ostinato character of its melody, and its modality, suggests Russian folk songs.

Example 29

(a) *Jenufa: Wedding chorus.*
(b) *Boris Godunof: Feodor's Song.*

A similar relationship is shown by the following two examples:

Example 30

   (a) *Kátà Kabanová: Kudrja's Song.*
   (b) *Boris Godunof: Song of the Gnat.*

The bell-motifs in *The House of the Dead* and in the *Glagolitic Mass*, too, seem to be shaped according to Russian prototypes.

Example 31. The House of the Dead, 2nd act, p. 66.

A much-discussed problem is that of form in Janáček's music. The objection has been made that Janáček's themes lack the capacity for intrinsic growth and thus of generating form in the strict sense of the word. According to this view, it is the purely mechanistic principle of repetition, variation, and contrast which is at the root of the composer's form. Critics maintain that thematic or modulatory developments in the manner of traditional classical and romantic instrumental music as well as polyphony and counterpoint, are absent.

It is true that little can be found of these devices in Janáček's music. His form-building principle consists in the transformation of a short idea which is kept flowing by melodic orchestral and rhythmic variation, or by the addition of new accompanying figures—one can hardly call them counter-voices in the contrapuntal sense. Frequently, an idea thus established is confronted by a contrasting character, which is either treated in the same way, or alternates, in Rondo fashion, with the first theme. Such a, as it were, two-dimensional, one-plane construction has its advantages. The melodic idea is brought home to the listener with the utmost possible intensity and plasticity, the theme preserving its vitality to the end in this unilateral process, while the pulverisation and attenuation of the melodic impulse that often occurs in a conventional development section, is avoided.

One of the mysteries of Janáček's originality and vitality lies in his treatment of themes. His formal structures rely on a melodic dynamism which neither pursues the driving power of rhythm and sound to be found in Stravinsky, nor the impression-istic principle of gliding harmony groups. The primal power of this dynamism is one of the undefinable qualities in Janáček's creativity. We can but divine this or that component of this primal power: the autonomous emotional origin of his melodies warrants their convincing veracity; their growth from folk music enhances the vitality and the elemental force of their character.

A typical example of an instrumental movement based on the principle of repetition and rhythmic variation is the prelude to the 2nd scene in the first act of *The Cunning Little Vixen* (p. 22). The principle of repetition operates here with such concentration and severe economy that this simple variation movement becomes imbued, throughout, with life and truth. The theme

Example 32

undergoes the following modifications:

Example 33

Fragments of the theme are used as accompanying figures in

the subsequent scene (dialogue of the vixen with the hunting dog), the wail of the vixen showing an interesting correspondence with the closing paragraph of the variation theme.

Example 34

It is quite evident that his special manner of formal construction is beset by certain dangers; all the more so since Janáček's melodic style is, as we realise, essentially miniaturistic. In short instrumental or vocal forms, particularly when words are joined with the melody, the vitality of invention is always maintained, and it is here that Janáček seems most convincing, as for instance in the song cycle *Diary of a Young Man who Vanished* or in the movements of the *Sinfonietta* that are constructed from short periods. But as soon as a melodic idea lacks this characteristic dynamism, Janáček's forms tend to give a fragmentary and forced effect, as in the first movement of *Taras Bulba* which, despite many original details, never quite begins to flow.

Janáček's harmony, too, has given cause for much critical discussion. In his early works, he has mostly followed the chromatic-enharmonic principles of late romanticism (*Idyll*, *Šárka*, etc.). Later, under the impact of modality, the whole-tone melodies and harmonic progressions of impressionism become frequent.

Example 35. The Cunning Little Vixen, 2nd act, pp. 66/67.

Chords of the Ninth and Seventh, in various positions and alterations, offer him the material for those dissonances which he needs for the harmonic characterisations of certain situations, especially in the operas. From these chords spring the sharp, grating seconds—his preference being for minor seconds—which abound particularly in the later operas (*The Makropulos Case, The House of the Dead*). The dissonant accompaniment of Suratov's grotesque song in the first act of *The House of the Dead* is based on these harmonic devices; it represents the maximum use of the dissonance to be found in Janáček's music.

Example 36. The House of the Dead, p. 36.

Under the impact of the harmonic idiom of contemporary European music, chords and melodies of the Fourth become increasingly frequent in Janáček's later works (*Sinfonietta, The House of the Dead, Second String Quartet*). There are also beginnings of polytonal structures, as in *The Cunning Little Vixen* and the *Second String Quartet*. Polyphony, however, is generally rare in Janáček's music. Most commonly, we find counter-voices that invigorate a main idea, and above all, copious figuration, often producing polyrhythmic structures.

Janáček's harmony was influenced, as we have seen in the preceding chapter, by his modal cast of mind. The freedom with which he employed modal progressions essentially signifies the limits of his harmonic "modernity". He has never left the realm of tonal composition, though he sometimes penetrated close to its borders. 'There is no music without key. Atonality abolishes definite key, and thus tonal modulation . . . Folk song knows of no atonality . . .[1]

Yet it is in his modulations, if anywhere, that Janáček has been most unorthodox. To be sure, the tonal instability of folk song exerts its influence even here. The harmonic instability and ambiguity of Eastern Moravian and Slovak folk melodies implies not so much modulation proper as rather the elaboration of a melody in a sphere of tonal freedom, a phenomenon that

[1]cp. Leoš Janáček, *O tónině v lidové písni* (Tonality in Folk Song). 1926.

is reflected by the apparent lack of harmonic logic in Janáček's music. A typical example of the vague, floating quality of his tonalities is the opening theme of the symphonic poem *Taras Bulba*. The melody is centred on F sharp minor, but sounds—and in Janáček's capricious spelling, also looks—like an atonal structure. The aeolian minor seventh, F flat (E), of the first bar, the augmented fourth B sharp (c), reminiscent of the gipsy scale, of the second bar, the phrygian minor second G of the third bar— these give the melody a strangely exotic, meditative character that points to the realm of expressionism.

Example 37

In the main, Janáček's modulations aim at the adjacent, only rarely at related, keys; thus, his harsh chord progressions between neighbouring keys are brought about (*The House of the Dead*, *Glagolitic Mass*, etc.).

Of his theoretical writings, which are in part founded on Helmholtz's 'Die Lehre von den Tonempfindungen' and on the psychological researches of Wundt, it was, first and foremost his theory of chord progressions that claimed attention.[1] One of his fundamental ideas is the law of the freedom with which chords may be combined and resolved. The simultaneous sounding of unrelated harmonies, or the immediate succession of such chords, is explained by him on the basis of acoustic-psychological experience. According to this, any chord will produce, immediately after being sounded, a reverberation lasting a tenth of a second (a tenth of the original sound volume), which will mix with the sound of the new chord. Owing to the capacity of this short reverberation for 'thickening' the new harmony, the harmonic character of the subsequent chord will strike the listener as the more distinct, and exciting the more it has sprung from a short moment of 'chaos'—the coincidence of the reverberation with the new harmony. The harsh chord progressions, as well as Janáček's abrupt modulations, find their explanation in this theory. Here is an example from the Gloria of the *Glagolitic Mass* of such a succession of chords reminiscent of Stravinsky.

Example 38

Objection is often made to Janáček's orchestration, and that with some degree of justification, for occasionally it is inadequate. The difficulties that attended the performance of his larger works

[1] *Structure and Progressions of Chords* ('Bau und Verbindung der Akkorde' 1897); a revised and enlarged version appeared (1920) under the title *Vollstaendige Harmonielehre*.

on this account were very real, and as we know,[1] it was for this reason that the Prague première of *Jenufa* was delayed by several years. Janáček's orchestral thinking was intimately wedded to the special character of his melodic-rhythmic invention. Individual and striking as his themes were, they demanded adequate instrumental colouring. This explains the many original touches in the orchestration of his instrumental movements, especially those frequent cases where instruments are used in an unfamiliar part of their range. Janáček was no practised hand in orchestration. His training in this field had been inadequate, and he himself has repeatedly and openly admitted this fact. But here again, he shows courage in doing justice to a vision that departs from convention, accepting hostile criticism rather than pursuing the trodden path.

In judging Janáček's scores, one must keep in mind that they are not laid down in accordance with the classical-romantic tenets of balancing the ensemble of the three orchestral families. He did not follow any conventional scheme of orchestration—just as his forms sprang from a spontaneous impulse for improvisation. This accounts for the frequent changes in the orchestral lay-out— every section seems to obey its own law of instrumental character- isation. This approach led to Janáček's unusual practice of dis- pensing more and more with ordinary, ruled manuscript paper, and, instead, ruling in by hand on an empty sheet as many staves as were needed for special sound effects. (See plate facing p. 129).

Characteristic of this, as it were, kaleidoscopic treatment of the orchestration is the *Sinfonietta:* here, the lay-out changes with every movement, and within the movements, interesting sound- effects follow each other at short intervals. This work is specially successful in point of orchestration, and apart from its numerous original details, as the combination of Piccolo, three flutes and

[1] cp. Ch. 6, p. 64.

low-lying trombone chords[1]—a contrast incidentally beloved of Janáček—the treatment of the wind is of an exquisite brilliance, particularly in the first movement and in the finale. The instrumental doublings so often met with in Janáček are conspicuously absent from this work, nor is the transparency of sound obscured by his usual rhapsodical accompaniment figures (*Taras Bulba*). Generally speaking, Janáček's scoring is characterised by primitive vigour and directness of colouring. He is fond of depicting descriptive details in characteristic instruments, as the clacking of the mill-wheel in *Jenufa* (xylophone); the grotesque action of the Don Juan scene in *The House of the Dead* is accompanied, amongst other instruments, by a rattle; in the love-scenes in *Kátà Kabanová* and *The Makropulos case*, the viola d'amour appears (originally this instrument was intended also for the *Second String Quartet*); bells in *The House of the Dead* and *The Cunning Little Vixen* produce a certain rustic solemnity; the popular appeal of the Hussite chorale in *Brouček* is underlined by bagpipes, etc. Janáček's partiality for the sound of the kettle-drum, particularly in connection with the brass, has already been noted.

Janáček's piano-writing, too, shows the uncompromising realism of his other works. Of all instruments, the piano was perhaps the one nearest to his heart. It was capable of rendering the rhythmic-melodic conciseness of his style, as well as the rhapsodical, impressionistic sound-images of his lyrical miniatures. His piano pieces (*On an Overgrown Path*, *In the Mist*) display, on an intimate scale, the structural and tonal characteristics of his larger conceptions. The same approach, but emotionally and texturally on a higher plane, is to be found in his *Piano Sonata 1. X. 1905*, while the piano-writing of Janáček's two late works, the *Concertino* (1925) and the *Capriccio* for the left hand (1926) clearly indicate a restraint pointing in the direction of chamber music.

[1] 3rd movement, p. 49.

CHAPTER 11

JANÁČEK'S OPERAS

Nationalism and patriotism, those generative forces of musical romanticism, have produced their finest fruits in the field of opera. The subject-matter is everywhere the same—national saga or the milieu of the plain people—whereas style and form display the greatest possible variety. The music-drama and the *Spieloper* of the Germans, the aria-form, and again, the *verismo* of Italian opera, the ardent realism of the Russians—they are the expression of a given historical situation and national disposition. Amongst the small nations, the Czechs have proved their brilliant national genius for opera with some of Smetana's works and Dvořák's *Rusalka*; at the same time it has been shown that theirs is an intermediary position between the Germanic, Latin, and Slavonic worlds. In some of Smetana's operas, i.e. *Dalibor* or *Libuše*, German influences (Wagner) are almost as strong as his Czech national style, based as this is on Italian and French conventions; Dvořák's operas are similarly conceived within the framework of their time; least noticeably so, perhaps, the typically Slav fairy-tale *Rusalka*. Janáček's position as a composer of national opera is, on the whole, clearer. In the first place, unlike so many musicians of his period, he is no cosmopolitan. As a man and an artist his culture is entirely Slavonic, with a strong leaning towards the Slavonic East; by origin, he is Moravian, i.e. he belongs to that strong, earthbound peasant-race that differs widely from the mundane and urbane civilisation of the Czechs in Bohemia. A successor of romanticism, and witness of the national awakening of his people, he was bound, almost by necessity, to find his way to opera.

Besides his nationalism and early romanticism there were, to be sure, other and deeper impulses that drove Janáček towards opera. Janáček's operas are the outcome of his profound understanding of the human soul and its reactions, of his perspicacity towards the most subtle meaning and expressive shades of human speech, of his well-nigh elemental affinity with Nature, of his conviction that he was a responsible participant in all everyday events of real life. The 'natural' musician derived his truest and strongest artistic impulses from his humanity and the sensuality which he sublimated into a philosophy. As the melody of speech opened to him 'a little window into the human soul', so the sounds of Nature and the voices of animals carried for him a secret meaning, and were manifestations of life. His experience of the Great Pan becomes the key to his dramatic-lyrical creativeness.

These are the roots of Janáček's dramatic *oeuvre*. To his impetuous temperament, his philosophy of compassion, and the vocal trend of his musical thought, opera was bound to become the most congenial form of expression. Janáček's stage-works are not born from any sensual or intellectual delight in music-making, nor do they strive towards the objectivation of a poetic idea or musical form. With him, everything is seen subjectively in the first place; his ideas have the freshness of spontaneous inspiration, and their artistic moulding obeys the logic of his impulsive mind. The inborn instincts of his genius are devoid of any literary or intellectual snobbery. Viewed superficially, Janáček's libretti may lack unity, and are certainly very diverse in character. If we consider two of his most characteristic works,

The Cunning Little Vixen and *The House of the Dead*, we must ask ourselves what were the considerations that prompted a dramatic composer to choose subjects of such obvious dramatic weakness.

What chiefly interested Janáček when choosing his texts was whether they offered a possibility for the emotional enlargement and psychological enhancement of certain states of the mind, even though these may at first have seemed incapable of dramatic development. The sensitivity of his speech-melody technique enabled him to give musical significance to every word and every gesture, with the result that contrasts of great effectiveness are achieved even in static situations. The passionate intensity of his a cappella choruses and the dramatic power of the opera *The House of the Dead*, where progressive action in the traditional sense does not exist, depend on this intrinsic dynamism of Janáček's style. Boldness and an element of the fantastic in a libretto seemed to stimulate his artistic inspiration; his music, delineating human speech as it does, seeks the out-of-the-ordinary, which is singularly able to disclose to him the heights and depths of the human soul and the mystery that lies at the back of all life.

The utter diversity of his operatic subjects throws an instructive light on Janáček's inner development. The romantic, conventional *Šárka* (1887-88), completed 1924, and the balladesque one-act opera *Beginning of a Romance* (*Počátek románu*, 1891) are followed by *Her Ward* (*Její pastorkyně*), better known as *Jenufa* (1895-1903), a village tragedy from Janáček's Eastern Moravian homeland. The conversational opera *Fate* (*Osud*, 1903-04), set in the urban milieu of the nineteen-twenties, forms the bridge to the fantastic burlesque *The Excursions of Mr. Brouček* (*Výlety pana Broučka* 1908-17). There follows the tragedy of adultery, *Kátà Kabanová* (1919-21), the quasi-pantomimic animal-opera *The Cunning Little Vixen* (*Liška bystrouška*, 1921-23), the symbolistic utopia *The Makropulos Case* (*Věc Macropulos*, 1923-25), and his last opera,

The House of the Dead (*Z mrtvého domu* 1927-28), which is infused
with Christian metaphysics. A motley array of subjects seemingly
chosen at random, and certainly inspired, to some extent, by
the artistic whimsicality of this unconventional musician. On
closer view, however, one finds that, with the possible exception
of *Beginning of a Romance* and *The Excursions of Mr. Brouček*,
Janáček in his operas pursues an inner line that is rooted in his
Slavonic ethos of compassion and his christian-pantheistic belief
in redemption. 'These splendid people'—he comments on
Dostoievsky's *Diary from a House of the Dead*—'suddenly something comes over them, and they have to suffer . . . They atone
for it, but they have hearts of gold.' 'Suddenly something comes
over them and they have to suffer . . .'—this is the motive,
repeatedly varied, of the guiltless guilty one, of a creature
overwhelmed by an elemental compulsion, of the *via dolorosa* as
an ordinance of creation itself—yet at the end there is redemption
and absolution. Jenufa, the unmarried mother who is abandoned
by her faithless lover; her guardian, throwing the fatherless child
into the brook; the adultery of the lonely, mentally enslaved
Kátà, and her atonement by committing suicide in the Volga; the
vixen that is overtaken by the hunter's bullet at the moment of her
greatest identity with life; the redemption of Elena Makropulos
from her 350-year-long existence by a diabolical experiment with
a life-elixir; the crimes of the condemned in the Siberian prison-
camp—'in every creature there is a divine spark' is what Janáček
said about these wretched existences—he approached all these
subjects not as a judge, nor as an objective observer, but as the
compassionate brother of all those imperilled and suffering beings.
In spite of all her sins, Kátà's soul is, 'as white as the surface of
the Volga in the moon light', and her guardian's criminal plan
of doing away with Jenufa's fatherless child in order to smooth
her path into the future, finds its higher justification: 'For God
Himself knows best that these things must happen.' Janáček's

Slav warmheartedness sheds over all guilt and punishment the rays of an all-embracing mercy.

It is interesting that most of Janáček's principal characters—and not only in his operas—are female. Šárka, the amazon of Czech legend, who, betrayed in love, takes bloody revenge on the male sex; Jenufa; the vixen; Kátà; Elena Makropulos. Here is a problem for the psychologist. The eroticist and pantheist Janáček, himself of masculine creativeness in all his actions, sublimates his experience of Eros: from all those figures, there arises transcendentally the timeless symbol of Mary Magdalen. Thus, his Slavonic naturalism, his eroticism and pantheism find their transfiguration in Christianity, and Janáček takes his legitimate place by the side of the great Slav-Christian seers, Dostoievsky and Tolstoy.

*   *   *

Jenufa is the first of Janáček's mature works for the stage. It is generally, and rightly, considered Janáček's *chef d'oeuvre*—the winning throw of a hitherto as good as unknown composer who has produced an unprecedented masterpiece, even as Athene sprang from the head of Zeus in radiant beauty and perfection. However, *Jenufa* had two dramatic precursors which, though unassuming, are stylistically not without interest: the mythological *Šárka* and the short popular opera *Beginning of a Romance*. Both works stem from that formative phase in Janáček's development when the composer had to come to terms with the artistic influences concerning him most closely. *Beginning of a Romance* is the distillation of his study of folk music, and in *Šárka*, Janáček's dependence on Dvořák and the music drama is irrefutable.

The romantic-national *Šárka* subject had already inspired Smetana to write his symphonic poem (1874) and was to be taken up again by Fibich in his opera of that name (1895); for a time (1878) Dvořák, too, had plans of setting Julius Zeyer's *Šárka* tragedy. In his patriotic enthusiasm, the thirty-three years old Janáček had selected Zeyer's Šárka as his first operatic subject; with the result, however, that Zeyer curtly prohibited the performance of this opera by an unknown composer who, moreover, had failed to obtain the poet's permission for setting the libretto. Janáček treated the text freely. It was to be his lifelong practice. He has to some extent freed the action (the tragic love of the nymph Šárka for the mortal prince Ctirad) from romantic and sentimental embellishments, stressing in his music the purely dramatic and lyrical elements. Echos of the *Leitmotiv*-technique as well as the colourful orchestration are proof of his dependence on Smetana and Dvořák, as also—and that quite strikingly—on Wagner, viz. the obvious affinity of the mytho-logical and symbolistic libretto to the Ring dramas. But it is astonishing how, on the other hand, at a time when the example of Wagner dominated the operatic life of his homeland, Janáček formed his own, realistically direct style, in opposition to the traditional idiom of the music drama (short motifs derived from speech inflection, next to ardently lyrical passages); how in certain melodic turns, particularly in the numerous choruses, he anticipates Dvořák's *Rusalka* of fifteen years later. Not until 1925 did *Šárka* have its first performance, in Brno; shortly before, the composer had subjected the work to a general revision. It was not a success, however, the uneven youthful effort does not hold its own against the well-known operas of Janáček's maturity.

The one-act opera *Beginning of a Romance* has an even less fortunate history. The action is based on a story by Gabriella Preissová, who was to be the authoress of the *Jenufa* text. It is a rustic love story, set in the Moravian peasant-milieu; it was set down in versified form by J. Tichý and used by Janáček in this form. The manuscript of the full score was lost for many years. After its performance in Brno in 1894, Janáček disowned the work, mainly because of the folk songs used in it—and in this

9

impulsive moment, some pages of the manuscript had even fallen victim to his severe self-criticism. But *Beginning of a Romance* is not a bad piece. The music is spontaneous, naive and warm-hearted, and the Moravian folk songs quoted here by the composer—this is the only instance when he incorporated existing melodies in his operas—in places lend the work the character of a *Singspiel*. Melodramatic passages exist side by side with Janáček's characteristic melodic and declamatory phrases; in fact, apart from the folk songs, Janáček's subsequent realism is strongly anticipated here. In his development as an opera composer, *Beginning of a Romance* signifies a decisive step towards the realistic and vernacular style of his major works; it is the connecting link between the romanticism of *Šárka* and the mature national opera *Jenufa*.

Jenufa is Janáček's first and fully representative operatic masterpiece. Text and action are modelled on Gabriella Preissová's drama of the same title, in which the authoress has successfully captured the heart-beat of the Eastern Moravian peasant-world. The plain motives of true vernacular drama are uplifted by Janáček's eruptive music into the sphere of the eternally humane. The notion of 'the people' means for Janáček—as, incidentally it meant for Smetana—something immeasurably chaste, nature-given, noble; nothing uncivilised, uncouth or vulgar. The conflict of the guardian who, out of love for her ward, does not shrink back from crime, is heroic and nothing short of the sublime. She is the most important character in the drama. Next to her, Jenufa appears more truly feminine; there is warmth and dedication in her, and again greatness which manifests itself in her forgivingness, and in her courage to start a new life at the side of her hitherto spurned but truly loving companion.

Janáček's technique, based on the melody of speech, is displayed most happily in *Jenufa*. The experimental stage that was still perceptible in the earlier operas is overcome here. How good he is at extracting vibrant, exciting, shattering music from the raw-material of life and feeling as it presents itself in speech-melodies! The score of *Jenufa* is full of thrilling moments that are not easily forgotten. The lyrical ebbing away of the first scene in the second act ('Good night, mother,' p. 108) with its tender, flowing orchestral melody is such a moment—a well-wrought pendant to the blissful, visionary piano piece *The Virgin of Frýdek*. Then again the half-crazed excitement of the guardian in her great scene before carrying out the child's murder (Act II, p. 139). After this feverish monologue, a dull, leaden Jenufa enters, oppressed by a foreknowledge of disaster ('Mother, my head is heavy', p. 146); she gradually rouses herself to feeling, to action—it is a famous example of the psychological and emotional flexibility of Janáček's music, lending, as it does, a well-nigh superhuman dramatic dimension to this climax of the opera. Or again the final duet ('They went away. Go now you, too', p. 244), inwardly translucent, remote in its modal colouring; one of the most inspired *arioso* passages ever conceived by Janáček. And again, there are simple, folk song-like passages as, for instance, the wedding-chorus (Act III, p. 208), the chorus of the recruits (Act I, p. 38), or the choral song, mentioned in another context ('Daleko, široko' p. 50), viz. Chapter 9, p. 93.

The principle of repeating certain words or short melodic phrases, so characteristic of the singing practice of Eastern Moravian and Slovakian folk music, is another effect used in *Jenufa* with much poetical and psychological subtlety. As, in folk song, heightened emphasis is given to a thought or a feeling by the repetition of single words or phrases—it often seems like an echo of preceding sentiments, which re-vibrates in the same word—so Janáček's repetitions of a melodic phrase, too, enhance its emotional content to a degree which language alone would be quite incapable of achieving. In *Jenufa*, where bewilderment, faint hopefulness and desperation are the basic emotions of most dialogues, this device is often profoundly moving. Thus, for instance, the moment when Jenufa waters her rosemary-plant while voicing her fear that, if it should wither, all 'the luck in the world would wither with it.' In the two statements of this meditative phrase and its gradual dying away, the entire tragedy of Jenufa is anticipated emotionally (Act I, p. 15).

The repetition of a phrase as a form-giving characteristic is also used frequently in *Jenufa* on a bigger scale. This applies chiefly to the orchestral introductions to the three acts of the opera, which are constructed in an extensive al fresco style. Broadly conceived themes of lapidary simplicity are variously repeated and transformed here. The dramatic effect of these interludes is produced by the inner dynamism of those themes and by the primitive and, as it were, elemental, logic of their musical development. One will look in vain for intricate motivic or contrapuntal work, and here one can hardly speak of modulations in the strict sense of the word. Janáček usually maintains the flow of such instrumental movements by simple inversions, augmentations or diminutions of the main subject, or by adding a second melodic idea that is treated in like manner. The primitive design of these orchestral movements that introduce the three acts of *Jenufa* by no means deprives them of musico-poetical associations; on the contrary, the expressive conciseness of the themes and their development increases the dramatic poignancy. Thus, Rosa Newmarch sees in the short prelude to Act I a piece of milieu-painting—the clacking of the mill-wheel, with the obligato xylophone motif above pizzicato basses.[1] Max Brod calls the unquiet prelude to Act II, which is based on an accompaniment of semiquaver-triplets, 'Restless perambulations of two women'; 'sad wedding-cheers' is the epigram for the introduction to the third act[2] that is based on a meaningful transmutation of the

[1]Rosa Newmarch, *The Music of Czechoslovakia*, p. 213.
[2]Max Brod, *Sternenhimmel*, p. 39.

A flat minor theme of the first act's quartet 'Every couple must bide its time of suffering' (p. 66).

Janáček has been reproached, often unjustly, for the lack of polyphony in his music. Yet wherever the dramatic situation demands he is quite able to make use of this device. His choruses testify to this, and the previously mentioned quartet 'Every couple ...' with its modal A flat minor, is a fugato-section of great impressiveness; here, the stark tonality and melancholy pathos form one of the most inspired passages of the opera. Janáček's ensemble-style is, however, not so much polyphonic in feeling as polyrhythmic; his frequent combinations of rhythmical and metrical formulas are, after all, a stylistic element of Moravian-Slovakian folk music. Thus, the episode of the rosemary-plant is in a distinctly polyrhythmic vein (p. 15); so is the ensemble-scene after the discovery of the child's body (Act III, p. 227), where in places three or four metrical motifs are combined.

Fate (*Osud*) with a libretto by Fedora Bartošová (the idea was suggested by the composer), proves to be a link—albeit lacking the independent strength of a representative work— between the earthy realism of *Jenufa* and the burlesque *The Excursions of Mr. Brouček*. It is a work of preparation and trans- formation; a stylistic study, one might say, and as such compar- able to *Beginning of a Romance*. The action, an artist's tragedy, takes place in the urban milieu of the nineteen-twenties and partly in the social ambience of Luhačovice, a Moravian spa frequently visited by the composer. It is probable that Janáček's acquaintance with Charpentier's *Louise* (Prague, 1903) has influenced the con- versational tone of *Fate*, which, in comparison with *Jenufa*, is rather smooth and stylised. Even here, however, we find moments of that passionate intensity of expression that had been the hallmark of Janáček's dramatic music since *Jenufa*.

On the occasion of the International Janáček Congress at Brno

(1958), *Fate* was given its first performance, some previous radio performances (the first in 1934, Brno) having provided us with an incomplete preview of this opera. The stage performance made a mixed impression. While the music is of undeniable beauty, particularly in some lyrical and dramatic passages, which seem to hold out the promise of the work's survival, the libretto, on the other hand, is confused and forced, and might prove a serious obstacle to the work's more general success.

The Excursions of Mr. Brouček is generally considered one of Janáček's less successful stage works.[1] The reason for this does not lie only in the close proximity of the opera to the composer's masterpiece, *Jenufa*. Even on its own merits, *Brouček* is a fairly weak work, mainly because its text was an unhappy choice in several respects. To assume, as some critics have done, that Janáček's gift was less at home in the comic genre, is surely a fallacy—one need only think of *The Cunning Little Vixen* and the comic scenes in *The House of the Dead*. Janáček would certainly have composed successful comic operas if suitable librettos had been forthcoming. The book of *The Excursions of Mr. Brouček* is weak; it lacks unity, veering, as it does from crude realism to fantasy, to parody, and abstraction, while never becoming truly intellectual and subtle in its humour.

In the first place, too many authors had lent a hand with the book. The piano-score mentions Victor Dyk and Fr. S. Procházka, the latter gave the definite form to the combined efforts of five *littérateurs*.[2] The figure of Mr. Brouček is an invention of the poet Svatopluk Čech (1846-1908), who in a series of satiric novels depicted the John Citizen of Prague as a paragon of philistinism, gross materialism, and moral indolence. Janáček's libretto is based on two of these novels: *Excursion of*

[1] All references to the opera—to the plot, to certain scenes, musical details, pages in the vocal score—are based on the first edition of *The Excursions of Mr. Brouček*, Univ. Ed., 1919.

[2] K. Masek, Z. Janke, Fr. Gellner, J. Mahen, and J. Holy.

Mr. Brouček to the Moon (1887) and *New, Sensational Excursion of Mr. Brouček, This Time into the Fifteenth Century* (1888).

The atmosphere of medieval Prague sets the tone for the realistic frame-work of the burlesque. At the foot of the romantic Hradčany castle, is situated the inn Vikárka, where the good Brouček is one of the 'regulars'. There he dreams after one drink too many that he is removed first to the moon, then into the fifteenth century at the time of the Hussite wars. The patrons of the inn, the verger and his daughter Malinka, the painter Mazal, various characters of the Prague artistic world, not to forget the landlord, Würfl, are transformed into denizens of the moon, and again into contemporaries of the Hussite religious wars. Actual persons become phantoms and allegories, which however, are not always accepted as such by Janáček ('. . . I declare that the people on the moon and in the fifteenth century are real people . . .' he once wrote). This disrupts in many places the unified line of his musical characterisation and deprives it of the necessary conciseness. Only Brouček's own reality remains unimpaired, and not only various ages and places, but above all, contrasting spiritual worlds, meet and clash in his adventures.

Originally, Janáček planned to set no more than the first part of the comedy[1], but his experience of the first world war, which roused hopes of a better future for the Czech nation, made the Hussite episode more topical for him. Thus, the second part came into being during seven months of the year 1917.

The two episodes of the comedy are very different in mood, content, and dramatic impact. Reality and dreams, burlesque elements and philosophical, political, and religious deliberations are mixed together, and it may well have been the thought that colourful musical differentiation would have to go with this, that in the first place prompted Janáček to set this text. The wealth of dramatic figures, and quick moving action gives the whole opera

[1]He actually worked at this section of the opera during the years 1908-1917.

a touch of the cinema, a fact of which the composer was well aware, and which is to some extent reflected in the mobility of the musical setting.

The opera begins with a prelude, in true *buffo* vein, with two playful popular themes and one broad lyrical subject. These themes underlie the scene at the inn, the lyrical motif being associated with the love between Mazal and Malinka (pp. 27, 32). The scenes on the moon are treated as impressionistic pictures. Vibrant pianissimo-motifs (piccolo, p. 44), widely separated harmonies, repetitions of high pitched notes (p. 90), tremolos, biting rhythms, polymetrical effects (pp. 108, 134), motifs of the fourth, shimmering sounds, produce the colouring customarily associated with 'astral' effects. Some movement is brought into the virtually static scenes by the insertion of choruses and ballets.

The two acts on the moon are parodies not only of Brouček and the world of vulgar contentment for which he stands, they are, even more, satires on the intellectualising and aestheticising vacuity of a certain category of Prague artists, with their poses and affected clichés. In the 'Temple of all Arts' (Act II), radiant with magical lights—every ray represents one artistic genre— Brouček has to give answer to the troublesome questions of the lunar beings. 'Tell us how you have served the eternal ideals of love, beauty . . .' thus at once they corner him in the first act (p. 50). This dialogue is accompanied by skipping figures, reminiscent of the prelude (p. 49-50), and whenever love is mentioned, Mazal's lyrical motif occurs (pp. 50, 53). Etherea's (Malinka's) delicate melody (p. 56), later used as a waltz (p. 61), adds warmth and radiance to this scene. The second act (p. 80) is introduced by a noble string melody in D flat major featuring a variation of the love theme. But here, too, the unreal and burlesque elements turn out to be of too little dramatic and musical significance. The witticisms of the dialogue appear forced, if not downright pallid and abstract; and again, as in the scene of the anti-vegetarians (pp. 133-139), of a crudeness and vulgarity that destroys the equilibrium of the whole. Janáček's music, which is best when depicting real people and real conflicts, does not get going and, despite some passages of first-rate inspiration, remains contrived rather than inevitable.

The Hussite episode has greater life and conciseness, dramatically as well as musically. Again we find Brouček surrounded by his boon-companions, who are now changed into followers of Jan Hus. But this time, more is at stake than quasi-moralistic and aesthetic questions. In the struggle during which the fate of the Czech nation was decided, Brouček is meant to play an honourable part. His last-minute defection is an event that gives a deeper meaning to the satire. It now becomes a warning to the dilatory, the easily contented and compromising members of his own nation—a sort of self-analysis and justification. This is why the composer dedicated the work to the liberator of the Czech people, T. G. Masaryk.

Next to some buffo-motifs resembling those from former scenes, we find here grand melodic-dramatic passages, such as the scenes of Kunka (Malinka, pp. 221, 251) culminating in her tragic song when she learns of the death of her father (p. 278). Her fervour and depth of feeling is like an echo from the world of Jenufa. The many choruses make the strongest possible impact, particularly where the belligerent crowd—in agreement with the historical Hus—sings its war-like chorales. The first act of the Hussite episode is dominated by one of these austere chorales in Janáček's special vein ('Harken, ye warriors of God' pp. 93, 198, 201); the second act contains the famous Hussite choral, 'Ye who are the warriors of God' in contrapuntal combination with the solo-melody of the Lord's Prayer (p. 254).

Janáček's profound affinity with the Russian world, accounts as we have seen, for a whole series of works and projects. Among his operatic output, *Kátà Kabanová* is the first and most important of these creations.

In pursuing the motif of guilt and punishment, its projection into a universal context, and the public penance and eventual purification and transfiguration of the sinner, Janáček has continually been drawn into the orbit of Russian emotional life and literature. His operatic projects dealing with Tolstoy's *Anna Karenina* and *The Living Corpse* are phases of this inner search; *Kátà Kabanová* and *The House of the Dead* are climactic works of assured mastery.

Kátà Kabanová is based on A. N. Ostrovsky's (1824–86) drama *Gruza* (Storm), a social critique of the world of Russian provincial businessmen and *petits bourgeois*. Janáček had already read the piece in the Russian original before it was given in Prague in a Czech translation (1919). As always, he changed the original structure of the play radically to meet his own ends, concentrating on the main dramatic argument, eliminating inessentials and telescoping Ostrovsky's five acts into three. With Ostrovsky, the study of manners takes pride of place; he describes the provincial middle-classes as being dominated by greed, class despotism, petty prejudice and moral and intellectual narrow-mindedness. Kátà's tragedy is merely a symptom, an episode, as it were, in this depressing panorama. With Janáček, Kátà's fate becomes the central point of the action, and her tragedy is uplifted into the realm of the eternally humane and symbolic. True nobility of heart and genuine capacity for love are here confronted with the merciless stupidity of meaningless conventions. It is the conflict between sterile lack of feeling and imagination on the one side, and creative love on the other; between an ossified and fanatical morality, and a pure heart that gives of itself unsparingly.

The evil Kabanicha, Kátà's mother-in-law, is the villain of the piece, the personified principle of absolute power, which she exercises not only over Kátà, but also over her weak-willed son Tichon. As in *Jenufa*, *The Cunning Little Vixen*, and in *The House of the Dead*, the composer passionately takes the part of the fallible creature, stigmatised by guilt. Kátà's soul is clean and innocent in a higher sense, and it is only under the irresistible pressure of her enslavement and loneliness that she gives herself to a kindred soul, Boris. Bliss of love is followed by a rapid collapse. Enervated by her previous mode of life, she cannot bear the thought of adultery. She confesses her sin in public, and after a visionary farewell from Boris, seeks peace in the waters of the Volga.

Musically, *Kátà Kabanová* is Janáček's most mature masterpiece. It is more concise in design than *Jenufa*, though scarcely richer in musical ideas. The characters are sharply drawn melodically; a number of associative motifs lend clarity and poetic logic to the action, and the orchestra is treated symphonically rather than rhapsodically. Here Janáček's stage idiom appears at the peak of its development; the scenic plan is terse and economical, leading up to the tragic crisis in an unbroken emotional crescendo.

Janáček's treatment of the motifs associated with certain characters or moods of the drama is of a consistency that calls to mind the technique of music drama itself. Yet there is an essential difference between Janáček's free technique and Wagner's rigorous *Leitmotiv*-style. With Janáček, these associative motifs are inserted into the flow of the scene in an entirely natural, improvisatory manner. They vitalise the scene as long as its inner dynamism demands this, and eventually abdicate in favour of the realistic accompaniment employed prior to their appearance. With Wagner, the *Leitmotiv* shapes an entire scene with inescapable logic; it becomes the dominant musical symbol, the common denominator of the scene, waxing and waning with the dramatic impulse, and weaving a symphonic-polyphonic web by way of comment. Janáček's themes, on the other hand, in their free, dynamic mould, maintain throughout the character of associative motifs, motifs of recollection, as it were, and that notwithstanding their multiform musical development and variation.

One of the main motifs of the opera appears as early as the prelude. It announces itself first as a hollow knocking rhythm on the kettle-drums, chiselling out the characteristic fourth F— B flat in pianissimo triplets—menacing, fateful, and eerie. Soon, it appears in new instrumentation (flutes, oboes) at Allegro speed; now it is a gay tune, depicting the tinkling of bells and the trotting of horses. It is the theme of Tichon's departure, illustrating the headlong rush of the *troika* into the far distance, at the same time indicating Kátà's isolation and loneliness. In various forms, this theme dominates the whole opera. We hear it at Tichon's farewell, first urgently and threateningly (pp. 54-56), then rapped out by oboes and violins *col legno* (p. 62), and again as a broadly tragic statement in A flat minor given out by the kettle-drums with superimposed trombone chords (p. 68). It erupts with shattering force in the third act when Kátà, during the raging thunderstorm, accuses herself of adultery (pp. 135-137); and lastly, after Kátà's body has been found and Tichon has hurled his accusation at his mother ('You have killed her . . .') it ends the opera as a tragic memento (p. 163).

From this motif of fate, two further motifs are developed, both belonging to the emotional world of Kátà. The more important of the two, in B flat minor, established in the first prelude (p. 8) by clarinets and violas, dominates the greater part of Kátà's dialogue with Kabanicha and the subsequent scene with Tichon (pp. 29-36).

Another leading motif appears: Kátà's gentle, heartfelt love-melody, first indicated in the prelude (p. 10) and fully stated in C flat major, Adagio, by the flutes (p. 27). Next to the fate-motif, this is one of the most important thematic statements of the opera. Its metamorphoses delineate most sensitively and flexibly the various phases of Kátà's destiny. Thus, for example, it is interwoven into the descriptive demi-semiquaver figure of the second scene in Act I (p. 37-38), that delicate instrumental movement which Janáček developed from the image of flying swallows ('Strange that we cannot fly as the little swallows do ...'), contrasting this with Kátà's loss of freedom. The emotional climax of this dialogue with Barbara, too (p. 50) is carried by this theme in rich harmonisation. We find it again in the interlude before the change of scene in Act II (pp. 86-87), before Kátà's meeting with Boris; it recurs freely remodelled, during the subsequent love-scene (pp. 97-108), culminating in a glorious vocal phrase of Kátà ('Ah, long have I known you,' p. 108); and it ends this scene in the form of weighty chords whose pathos is reminiscent of Puccini (p. 112).

The secondary figures of Kudrjaš and Barbara are important links in the action, and have, therefore, been given increased musical stature by Janáček. They are popular characters, contrasting with the heroic couple, and their musical idiom is fresh, light, and adapted to the Russian vernacular. The gay motif of Barbara expresses 'transparent, rational sensuality'[1] (p. 51); it is strongly exposed in the scene where she persuades Kátà to hold her secret meeting with Boris (p. 74); and again in her duet with Kudrjaš ('Wanja is calling from the other bank ...', p. 93). She is the temptress, not out of wickedness or ill-will, but rather wantonness and impulsiveness. Her motif appears once more, as accompaniment to Kudrjaš's song 'Everyone is going home ...' (p. 110). This good-tempered Kudrjaš presents himself with three light-hearted folk songs which do not disguise their Russian origin (pp. 87, 94, 110). Kabanicha's aggressive motif of a seventh has been already mentioned (cp. Chapter 10, p. 109).

The choruses are reduced to a minimum in *Kátà Kabanová*. As in *The House of the Dead*, their principal function is to establish

[1]cp. Max Brod, *Leoš Janáček*, p. 49.

a mood. Eerie sounds surround Kátà's wordless melismata from afar (Adagio, p. 145), which subsequently, before her suicide, will rise up like sighs from the Volga (pp. 158-160). Time and again, we find in Janáček these personified, demonised utterances of Nature (*The Cunning Little Vixen*, *The Diary of a Young Man who Vanished*, etc.).

If we suppose that every opera of Janáček in turn reveals to us a different aspect of his personality (and humanity), then *The Cunning Little Vixen*, this most remarkable and individual stage-work, will compel our attention to a special degree. The keen-eyed, sensual composer ventures here upon a charming game of transmutations, a world suspended between man and beast. The shades of animal darkness extend into the daily sphere of human activity and officialdom. The huntsman, the parson, the school-teacher, the poacher, the forester's wife—they all become drawn into the mysterious twilight of Eros which penetrates every word of the action and every bar of the music. Nowhere is Janáček as free, as true to himself as in this opera; nowhere does he reveal himself more intimately than in those frank dialogues which lift the veil from the heart's most private concerns. The native charm of these scenes of nature is quite unique. With serene artlessness and with profound belief in the oneness of all creation, Janáček here bears witness to the great god Pan. He who was so deeply engrossed with the rhythms of Nature and the law of animal life, reveals here his own commitment to them, his identification with the earth and its beings.

The action—if this is not too pretentious a word for these impressionistic scenes based on a fable of Rudolf Těsnohlídek—is soon told. The huntsman has fostered at his dwelling a young orphaned fox cub, but one day it runs off to the woods—it is now strong and old enough to obey the law of its own nature. Soon enough, this law takes its course. Spring brings love and pairing; there follows the happiness of motherhood, and now, at the peak of fulfilment, surrounded by her cubs, the vixen is struck down by the poacher's bullet.

In this animal-opera, symbolic elements are worked out more clearly than in any other stage work by Janáček. The vixen is the centre of the plot, the magnetic pole in whose field all the other figures move, the symbol of eternal motherhood. She is sensual, coquettish, sly, loving—motherly. The aura emanating from her womanliness seizes and bewilders human hearts. The huntsman is under her spell; and in a grotesque nocturnal scene, when the vixen, hidden behind a sun-flower, watches the school-teacher and the parson returning to their homes, these men, too, come under the spell of her iridescent presence, and in self-revealing monologues confess their secret desires and memories. How graceful and chaste is the description of the vixen's first encounter with her mate! The love scene in the nocturnal forest is the climax of the opera. It is the magical signal for the wordless, uprushing hymn in which the beasts of the forest, and also the forest itself, lift up their voices. An epithalamium on a bell-motif, concludes one of the most impressive scenes in all Janáček's music.

The supremacy of rhythm in this opera is occasioned mainly by the frequent descriptive and onomatopoeic nature-motifs which form the basis of the melodic invention. In the animal voices and the ballet scenes of the animals, rhythm is a primary motivating force. Thus, the first act opens with a symphonic pantomime; a web of sounds and animal voices in the warmth of the summery forest. The blue dragon-fly hovers above an elegant, lyrical waltz tune (p. 6); cricket and grasshopper move in a syncopated polka rhythm. (p. 9). A naively grotesque waltz of indefinite tonality accompanies the first entry of the young vixen (p. 15). Frequently, the rhythm is condensed into polyrhythmic structures, as in the love scene where four-beat and irregular metres are combined with a fundamental three-beat

metre (p. 104, or pp. 108-109). The occasional whole-tone
melodies occurring here, point to late-romantic influences. An
interesting example with polyrhythmic implications is found in
the dialogue of the parson and school teacher at the inn (pp. 66-67).
The self-important clumsiness of the two men, fumbling and
bumbling under the influence of drink at a late hour, is presented
with amusing realism.

The lyrical element in *The Cunning Little Vixen*, however, is
by no means overshadowed by the stress Janáček lays on melodic
and rhythmic realism. Janáček's personal and artistic sympathies
are entirely on the side of the young vixen—the amatory,
elemental model of eternal womanhood. He has provided the
principal figure with a broad lyrical melody which first appears
in the instrumental interlude (A flat minor) leading into the
second scene of Act I. The theme undergoes several variations
here (p. 22), and in the intermezzo entitled 'The vixen's
femininity' (p. 34), it is eventually established, in luxuriant
orchestration, as one of the leading motifs of the opera. Another
important motif develops out of a vocal phrase ('Ach', p. 53)
of the vixen, somehow alluding to her experiences of love and
suffering (Cp. also Ch. 10, p. 109). It appears tellingly in the scene
of the sun-flower, as the accompaniment to the love monologue
of the teacher (p. 79), and of the parson's pensive (and almost
erotic) reminiscences from his early days (p. 80-81); the fantastic
scene is powerfully concluded by this motif (p. 87). It appears
once more in the scenes of the poacher Harašta, this time changed
into a quintuplet (pp. 139, 141, 154). Harašta's short song (p. 153)
grows out of its initial interval of a second; lastly, the vixen's
motif dies away in the pianissimo Adagio that follows her violent
end (p. 159).

After the tragic pathos of *Kátà Kabanová*, this opera was a work
of relaxation for the composer. The woods of his homeland
with their human and animal inhabitants were a familiar scene

to him into which he could easily place his charming, fantastic fairy-tale. Everything here is seen under the sway of the Great Pan. Man and beast coalesce in the fundamental unity of life. The huntsman and the vixen are the figures most precisely characterised. They are the principal characters, psychologically and oecologically they complement each other. In the secondary figures, the interchangeability of man and beast is demonstrated: the parson is identified with the badger, the teacher with the midge, the forester's wife with the owl; their parts are played by the same actors. Above the all-pervading, glowing eroticism and the refreshing humour of the work, there stands the great, eternal motif of Life and Death—so movingly revealed in the forester's final monologue (p. 172)—fashioned by Janáček into a deeply stirring, symbolic play.

Janáček's apparently arbitrary choice of his opera texts is perhaps nowhere as conspicuous as in *The Makropulos Case*. Nowhere has he stepped so far outside the range of subjects that are founded in the human and vernacular as in this setting of Karel Čapek's (1890-1938) comedy where reality and Utopia mingle with each other. It seems as if Janáček, at certain stages of his development, was unable to resist the lure of experimentation—*Brouček* and *The Cunning Little Vixen* had already been such deviations from convention and to a certain extent, *The House of the Dead* belongs to the same category. Janáček's volatile temperament was kindled by the strangeness of such subjects—and unpredictable as he was in the choice of his libretti, so it appears that in the experimental works his artistic success becomes most questionable.

What is *The Makropulos Case?* Karel Čapek, the first writer to put a robot on the stage, invents a fantastic plot that turns on a mysterious woman, Emilia Marty, alias Eugenia Montez, Ellian McGregor, Elsa Mueller, Ekaterina Myškin, correctly Elena Makropulos, a person who, being the daughter of the Emperor

Rudolf II's (1552-1612) body-physician and court-alchemist, has fallen victim to an experiment with a life-elixir, and is now condemned to live for four centuries. An involved legacy-suit eventually establishes her origin and sheds light on the strange events of her fantastic existence. Not before she has regained the magic formula of her immortality is she able to find her longed-for redemption in death.

On the face of it, this is not a bad operatic subject: the super-human figure of a woman without passion, love or human feelings, with the 'desiccated heart of a robot'[1] beside whom the other figures seem pitiable puppets. But the three acts are cluttered by so much argument and so many complications arising from the past, that the dramatic concision of the action suffers under this excess of dialectics. However, even in the figure of Elena Makropulos, Janáček expresses an eternal human issue— the wish for redemption—and in these lyrical moments his music appears most inspired. Nevertheless, Janáček's music was scarcely able to combat the weakness of the libretto. His setting loses itself for long stretches in a declamatory *al fresco* style, from which an occasional musical climax arises. The unreality and intangibility of the subject inhibits in the composer the lively inspiration of his folk operas, and the absence of the Slavonic element deprives his musical invention of national colour and vitality.

All the same, *The Makropulos Case* is technically one of the most mature works of Janáček. Only a great opera composer could have fitted these musical nuances within the dramatic framework, could thus have differentiated between melodic and declamatory phrases, could have piled up those towering climaxes of sound, and then again kept the texture flowing.

The extensive prelude to the first act contains two melodic characters: a lively fanfare-like motif that is to be played by trumpets and horns behind the scene and alludes to the far-off

[1] Cp. Fr. Pala, Janáček, Věc Makropulos, p. 5.

centuries of Elena's existence. It recurs when Elena's father is being mentioned (p. 160); with great lyrical emphasis in pianissimo chords when Elena recounts how the elixir had been tested on her when she was a girl of sixteen (p. 173); and at the end when her identity is being proved (p. 191). The other motif, a chordal structure of fourteen bars (p. 6), is one of the few lyrical periods in the opera connected with the human reactions and associations of the heroine. Belonging also to her sphere is an expressive lyrical motif (p. 22) which signifies the eeriness and sinister radiance of Elena Makropulos and which is subsequently played by a viola d'amour during Elena's scene with the lawyer Kolenatý (pp. 33, 35). The emphatic Makropulos motif (pp. 93, 124, 129, 153) is another character in this chain of musical symbols alluding to the super-natural. By contrast the angular motif of Kolenatý (pp. 30, 36, 48, 148, 176) outlines the lawyer's obliging correctness, whilst Albert Gregor, one of Elena's suitors, in fact, however, one of her offsprings, is characterised by an impulsive melodic gesture (pp. 58, 118).

Such leading and secondary motifs lend musical coherence to the action. Closed song-like sections, such as we find in *Jenufa* and *Kátà Kabanová*, are almost totally absent in the *Makropulos Case*. An exception is the quasi-exotic dance song of Baron Hauk (p. 98), one of the former lovers of Elena Makropulos. He had known her as a Spanish woman under the name Eugenia Montez. In general, Janáček's style in this penultimate opera is more astringent and ascetic than in his previous works. Dissonances are used increasingly as a means of dramatic expression, particularly when the horror of Elena's fate or the icy cynicism of her character are described (pp. 105, 107). Another characteristic feature of this opera is the verbal declamation, which is for the most part realistic, and frequently of ruthless harshness and almost expressionistic concentration. At the end, to be sure, a marvellous, conciliatory string melody transfigures this three-act nightmare (p. 181) and the opera dies away with Elena's blissful words: 'Wonderful, the tender hand of death on me.'

Janáček's last work for the stage can be called an opera only by a stretch of imagination. In the first place, there is no action in the ordinary sense, there are no female characters, and the main-spring of the dramatic tension lies in the past, as revealed in the tragic self-accusations and confessions of the convicts of a Siberian penal settlement. *The House of the Dead* is one of the most thrilling and, paradoxically, most vital operatic works of Janáček. Out of the tormenting present of the prison with its degradations and despair, vistas open onto the former life of single individuals; shattering panoramas of passion, aberration, and crime. This fateful knot, in which past and present are tied together, is the cause of the work's extraordinary intensity and overwhelming immediacy. The dynamism of a collective exper-ience, the impact of a tragic situation, is engendered in this community choked with guilt and misery.

From Dostoievsky's diary, which he kept as a political prisoner in Siberia (1850–54), Janáček has chosen some vivid, emotionally powerful episodes, freely adapting them to his dramatic needs. What captivated him most in these psychologically interesting reports, was the motive of guilt and the possibility of atonement and justification *sub specie aeternitatis*. 'In every creature there is a divine spark'—according to this motto of Janáček his artistic treatment of the subject is based on the contradistinction of human misery, brutalisation, and depravity on the one hand, and Slavonic-Christian piety which forgives and redeems the sinner, on the other. In spite of their utter degradation and despair, there exists a chance of salvation for all these prisoners.

Janáček's musical style in *The House of the Dead* corresponds to this philosophical standpoint. Next to violent dramatic out-bursts, we find lyrical scenes of great warmth and depth; one could even maintain that in no other work for the stage is

Janáček's realism permeated by such lyrical effusion and fervour. Here is the mellowness of a late work, the reconciliation with the all-too-humane, the far-ranging eye of a wise and benign exponent of the human heart—in fact, the quality that is found in Beethoven's last quartets.

Atmosphere reigns supreme in this opera. From a milieu that is made up of fear, cruelty, and cynicism—hardly relieved by the grotesque crudeness of the two pantomimes performed by the convicts—the images of human tragedies arise like a lightning flash through the night. In every act, the fate of one of the prisoners is unrolled. The drama is centred on three murders and three characters—Luka Kusmič, Skuratov, and Šiškov. The one is erratic, sadistic, and monstrous in his actions; the other simply impulsive, the victim of insane jealousy; the third emotionally unstable and therefore tending to extreme reactions.

With his gift for psychological characterisation, Janáček has firmly established the musical individuality of these three principal characters. Luka's narration is supported by broad declamatory lines; the music of his story is rich in expressionistic gestures, spiced with dissonances and grotesque rhythms (p. 42-55). By comparison, Skuratov appears in a warmer and gentler light. Janáček provides his tale with a lyrical melody which is one of the best passages of the opera (p. 73). Šiškov's theme is sombre and powerful; it first appears in modal form in the prelude to the third act (p. 120), and is subsequently varied, in differing tonal and rhythmical shades (pp. 141, 146, 149). By way of contrast to these 'lost souls' Janáček took over two more characters from Dostoyevsky's memoirs, the warmhearted, educated Alexander Petrovič and the gentle, almost maidenly, youth Aljeja. While the first three, together with the sadistic commandant, represent the Dantësque Inferno of *The House of the Dead*, Petrovič and Aljeja carry the banner of hope in a new life of freedom. A wounded eagle nursed by the prisoners becomes their symbol of

freedom. His harsh but proud theme (p. 25) occurs in the choruses
('Czar of the forest is he ...' p. 28-29) and in the poetical orchestral
interlude of Act III (p. 137) it forms a contrast to the marvellous
instrumental duet that precedes it, and in which peace and hope
are reflected. The motif of freedom which first appears in the
prelude to the third act (p. 121) and is to grow to full, triumphant
stature in the third scene (p. 190), where not only the eagle but
also Alexander Petrovič receive their liberty, also belongs to the
sphere of the eagle-theme. The poetic contrast to this solemn,
triumphal chord-motif—musically grown on the same stem—
is found in the sombre (A flat minor) Intrada theme which opens
the prelude to the first act—an important theme which is repeatedly quoted as a memento for the harshness and inexorability
of *The House of the Dead* (pp. 50, 146) and cast in the form of a
march (p. 68). The overture to the first act has found an
occasional place as a self-contained piece in programmes of
contemporary music. It is a typical example of Janáček's free
instrumental style with its strong contrasting groups. The Intrada
theme is varied here in many ways and relieved, in rondo style,
by alternating episodes. One of these episodes, the Allegro-
Presto (p. 2-3) was taken over by the composer from an unfinished violin concerto (1927-28) entitled *Pilgrimage of the Soul*
(Putování dušičky); the brilliant instrumental solo-part is
eloquent evidence of this.

Janáček's artistic relation to the Russian world is, of course,
much in evidence in *The House of the Dead*. Musical as well as
psychological elements underline the Russian atmosphere. The
choruses, for instance, are conceived not so much dramatically
as pictorially, and their melodic lines often closely approach to
related types in Moussorgsky and Borodin. Various arioso
passages, too, have a Russian flair, as Skuratov's little song (p. 32)
or his dancing song (p. 38-39). We have already mentioned the
various bell-motifs (cp. Chapter 10. p. 113). Russian popular say-

ings and adages are frequently quoted; thus 'Ere the devil brought us together he used up six pairs of shoes', 'Little birds, sharp claws', 'A black horse stays black though you may rub it with chalk', 'In spite of all our sins, we are still alive', etc. The feature, however, which most closely reflects the Russian concern with purification and redemption, is the ending of *The House of the Dead*; this goes also for the endings of *Kátà Kabanová*, *Jenufa* and, to a certain extent, of *The Makropulos Case*. They signify forgiveness and expiation, attained by deepest suffering in which the sinner's soul has been cleansed of his failings.

As we have noted in another context, Janáček's last opera was subjected to many textual and musical alterations. Most of these dealt with the orchestration, the elimination of crudities from the text, the remodelling of the scenario, and the rewriting of the finale. The final seventeen bars of the opera were inserted by O. Zitek[1] and B. Bakala[2] in place of Janáček's original version of the end of final scene which was totally different in style and mood. This conventional apotheosis of freedom had not been planned by Janáček. In accordance with the fundamental realism of the opera the work should have closed, after the exit of Petrovič and the flying off of the eagle, with a sharp call to order, summoning the prisoners to harsh reality from their dream of freedom, followed by their uneasy chorus ('Hou, Hou . . .'), and an orchestral epilogue of twenty-seven bars. Only a fleeting glimpse of freedom was to reach the prisoners—afterwards the House of the Dead should receive them again. In the Zitek-Bakala version, the opera closes on a false note, as it were. Janáček would have felt the repeated choral passages 'Day of happiness, day of freedom . . .' to be a sort of anti-climax; he was by no means intent on writing a triumphant finale based on cheap operatic

[1]Stage director and producer of the National Theatre in Brno.

[2]Pupil of Janáček who conducted the first performance of the opera in Brno (12th April, 1930) and carried out together with O. Chlubna, the musical alterations to the work.

convention. We publish here Janáček's original version of the end of the last scene. (See example on page 152.)

CHAPTER 12

CHORAL WORKS AND SONGS

JANÁČEK'S INTEREST in choral music extended over all phases of his creative activity. This is but natural if one considers the vocal origin of his music, and if one remembers his close connection with Pavel Křižkovský who takes great credit for the emergence of a Czech choral music inspired by the national spirit. Křižkovský, Janáček's teacher in the days of his stay at the Old Brno Augustine Abbey, is better known in Czech musical history for his choruses than for his church compositions. Breaking with the sentimental, pseudo-popular song cycle tradition of the *Liedertafel*-type, his choral style pulsates with the true life-beat of folk song; his melodies are adapted to the spirit of folk song, being at times astringent, at others of an earthy innocence and purity. These qualities, as well as his occasional leaning toward realism, show Křižkovský as a precurser of our master.

In our discussion of Janáček's attitude to folk music (cp. Ch. 9, pp. 92-95), we have already noted the various phases of his early choral style. It is important to realise that it was through the medium of choral writing that his style changed from the formalistic classicism of his youth to the vernacular realism of his maturity. In the setting of folk song texts, the problems of his speech-tone style presented themselves, in their full force. The intonation and metre of these poetic models, together with their emotional values, which were ethnically and regionally specified, provided his inspiration with a clearly defined artistic framework. To fill this framework, as it were, with its own, congeneric music, was a task for which Janáček was highly qualified at the beginning of the 1870's.

His first choral works—partly arrangements of folk songs such as *Ploughing* (*Oráni*), in the main, however, his own settings of folk song texts—already show this new orientation.

In the years 1873-6, eight male choruses[1] appeared, written for the choral Society *Svatopluk* where Janáček was conductor. In their dramatic power, lyrical tenderness, harmonic astringency and rhythmical freshness, these are some of the earliest manifestations of a new artistic spirit.

In accordance with the uneven number of syllables in the text, the choruses *Inconstant love* (*Nestálost lásky*), *True love* (*Láska opravdivá*), *You will not escape fate* (*Osudu neujdeš*) are notated in free rhythm and without time-signature (cp. Ch. 9, pp. 92-93). In its lilting folksong rhythm, and even more in its bold modulatory structure, the chorus *Forsaken* (*Osamělá bez těchy*) points towards another, later version of this piece. The year 1877 saw the writing of the *Festive Chorus*, dedicated to the memory of Komenský— a conventional work of representation. The chorus for mixed voices *Autumn Song* (*Píseň v jeseni*, 1880) composed for an anniversary celebration of the Beseda, the political social club of the Czechs in Brno, is of a similar character. The hitherto unpublished male chorus *Elegy* (*Zpěvná duma*, 1876) and the folkloristic *Wild Duck* (*Kačena divoká*, 1885), intended for a school song-book, were also written in those early days.

The next group, four male choruses published in 1886 and dedicated to Antonín Dvořák, already show Janáček's characteristic dramatic expressiveness. *Warning* (*Vyhrůžka*) is based on

[1]*Ploughing* (*Oráni*), *War-song* (*Válečná*), *Inconstant love* (*Nestálost lásky*), *Forsaken* (*Osamělá bez těchy*), *How strange my lover is* (*Divín se milému*), *The fading wreath* (*Vínek stonulý*), *Láska opravdivá* (*True Love*), *Když me nechceš, což je víc?* (*If you don't want me...*)

the variation of a two-bar motif which in its modifications reaches an exciting dramatic climax; *O love* (*O Lásko*) is a jolly little song in 7/8 time whose melodic accents fall on the weak beats, thus creating a piquant effect of blockages within a flowing melodic movement. *War, war* (*Ach vojna, vojna*) develops a harsh declamatory melodic-rhythmic formula, thus conjuring up the frightening image of war and terror that oppresses the drafted recruit. By way of contrast, the last chorus *Your beautiful eyes* (*Krásné oči tvé*) maintains a more gentle, lyrical note.

A further group, belonging to the year 1904 and published under the title *Four Moravian choruses* (*Čtvero mužských sborů moravských*), approaches, in its frequently gay character, the mood of *The Excursions of Mr. Brouček*. The most popular numbers of this collection are the meditative, and yet ardent, love song *Now you know* (*Dež víš*), and the nimble nature-piece *The gnats* (*Komáři*) with its sorties into the grotesque and exotic. Roguish humour permeates *The Witch* (*Klekánica*); *Farewell* (*Rozloučení*) is sorrowful, dark, inexorable.

The peak in the range of Janáček's unaccompanied male choruses is formed by the three ballads *Kantor Halfar* (1906), *Maryčka Magdonová* (1906/7) and *Seventy thousand* (1909)—they reveal unique flashes of genius in their emotional dynamism and bitter social critique. The texts are by Petr Bezruč, a poet from the Moravian-Silesian industrial area with whose philosophy and poetic diction Janáček had much in common (cp. Ch. 7, p. 74). His theme is the misery of the workers who live in the black country of smelting works and coalmines around Moravská Ostrava and Vitkovice. Their bloodless faces tell of social exploitation, unrelieved poverty—a Slav variant of Zola's *Germinal*—and national suppression; it was here that the national ambitions of Germans, Czechs and Poles clashed in bitter strife. The explosive tension of Bezruč's verses is translated dramatically into music by Janáček: we experience the eruption of a national group (*Seventy thousand*), and the catastrophes descending on an individual (*Kantor Halfar, Maryčka Magdonová*); from the grim harshness of reality, there arises, as always with Janáček, the conciliatory glow of compassion.

Kantor Halfar is the tragedy of national intolerance. This little, quiet man, the teacher Halfar, who is deprived of his livelihood because of his Czech nationality, has fallen on unhappy days and takes his own life; Maryčka Magdonová, a mother to her orphaned family, persecuted by the brutal authorities, chooses the same end.

What gives these choruses their uncanny, irresistible power is, apart from the obstinate driving-force of Janáček's melodic motifs, the bold, realistic technique of their development. Max Brod speaks of a peculiar union between 'clearest constructive force and elemental cry' as lending these choruses their 'irresistible dramatic impact'.[1] In *Kantor Halfar*, the inexorable 4/4 movement is relieved by the frequent metrical disengagement of the secondary parts, especially where the composer repeats sections of a verse, combining these with the normal flow of the strophes. These simultaneous motivic fragments help to create a poly-melodic and polyrhythmic feature of uncanny power. This principle is used most impressively in *Maryčka Magdonová*. Here Janáček calls forth the vision of an excited crowd, taking up the various phases of the drama, repeating them in different ranges and textures, even shouting them out, while the other voices continue with the steady progress of the narration. The melodic-harmonic-rhythmic counter-stresses resulting here are often of powerful acerbity, and bold dissonances enhance the weird realistic effect. In another context (Ch. 10, p. 107), I have mentioned the marvellously poetical end of the single strophes with their melodically expanded C sharp major cadence.

In *Seventy thousand*, this style is, if anything, enhanced by the

[1]Max Brod, Leos Janáček, p. 55.

158   LEOŠ JANÁČEK

theme of mass revolt which forms the basis of the story. As with *Kantor Halfar* and *Maryčka Magdonová*, *Seventy thousand* is cast in free rondoform, based in the main on the variation principle. The steadily rising emotional crescendo increases the complexity of the texture and eventually arrives at a wild paroxysm of passions—a momentous *al fresco* vision that seems to drown every detail. And yet this chorus too is constructed with a fine eye for detail; thus, the motif of 'May we live', first established by the solo-quartet, subsequently returns suspended above the other voices like a fanatical memento; and again, the menacing bass formula 'Marquis Gero' that forms the poetical and vocal contrast to the above motif, is built up into a similar quasi-ostinato function.

The performance of these choral works presents obvious difficulties of intonation, dynamics, grading of entries, etc. *Seventy thousand* was at first considered wholly unsingable, until the energetic Ferdinand Vach and his Choir of Moravian Teachers adopted the work and gave many memorable performances.

The *Songs of Hradčany* (Hradčanské písničky) for female chorus with flute and harp, and the ballad *Kašpar Rucký*, also written for female chorus and solo soprano, are imbued with Janáček's mood of patriotism during the first world war. As his artistic ambition continually looked towards Prague, he saw—not unlike Smetana in this respect—some symbolic significance in many of the capital's historic localities. The tenderly melancholic *Songs of Hradčany* (1916) reflect the legendary associations, and the poetry that surround the venerable Prague castle and the romantic, quiet streets, squares, palaces and gardens adjacent to it. In three mood-pictures of the most tender lyrical reticence and happiest melodic invention—*The Golden Street* (Zlatá ulička), *The Weeping Fountain* (Plačící fontána) and *Belveder*—Janáček has created a little treasure of vocal chamber music. The world's repertoire of music for female choir will one day be enriched by these valuable discoveries.

The ballad *Kašpar Rucký* (1916), too, is laid in the legendary Hradčany castle of Prague. This is the fantastic story of the alchemist Rucký, a wicked charlatan who lost his soul to the devil. After his violent end, numerous evil embodiments of himself swamp the imperial court—"New jesters jest on"—while he himself rides through the night on a fiery goat.

Musically, Janáček strikes here a tone of grotesque gaiety, suggesting comparison with *The Excursions of Mr. Brouček*. As in all his mature choral works, the part-writing in *Kašpar Rucký* is of emphatic individuality; not that Janáček creates a contrapuntal texture, but he freely combines a number of realistically conceived melodic lines. The contemporaneous female chorus *The Wolf's Track* (*Vlčí stopa*, 1916) is in a similar style; a balladesque piece composed to a text by Jaroslav Vrchlický.

From the end of the World War (1918) we have the male chorus *The Czech Legion* (*Česká legie*), a piece of great force and patriotic exultation. Kindred compositions are *Our Flag* (*Naše vlajka*, 1926), for male chorus and two sopranos, and the *Festive Chorus* (*Slavnostní sbor*, 1928) written to celebrate the laying of the foundation stone of the Faculty of Law building at the Brno Masaryk University.

A choral work of larger dimensions and greater artistic stature is *The Foolish Tramp* (*Potulný šílenec*, 1922) for men's voices and soprano solo to a text of Rabindranath Tagore. In somewhat unusual guise, this poem deals with an eternal human dream which fits in well with Janáček's philosophy of compassion: the search for the philosopher's stone, which makes man overlook the happiness that is near at hand. Janáček's music, in its mood and character, closely approaches the tone of the poem. The voices have individual dramatic life, in places, perhaps, excessively so, and to the detriment of the structure. All in all, however, this is a moving and inspired work.

Of lesser artistic and biographical importance are the male

choruses *Our Birch Tree* (*Což ta naše bříza*, 1893), *Little Wreath* (*Vínek*, 1893), *The Sun has Risen* (*Už je slunko z tej hory ven*, 1894, with tenor solo), *The Featherbed* (*Peřina*, 1914), a popular and humorous little piece; also the mixed chorus *Our Song* (*Naše píseň*, 1890), and the popular choruses from the ballet *Rákocz Rakoczy*, *When we Went to the Fair* (*Ked sme šli na hody*), *The Gnat's Wedding* (*Komáři se ženili*) and *Zelené sem sela*. The tragic pathos of the *Jenufa* period is reflected in the *Elegy*, a work for mixed chorus inspired by the death of Janáček's daughter Olga.

One of the peaks in Janáček's vocal writing is represented by the monodrama *Diary of a Young Man who Vanished* (*Zápisník zmizelého*, 1917-19). In a Moravian village, an honest peasant-lad disappeared one day without leaving a trace. Investigations remained fruitless, until a series of poems was found among the papers of the lost man, which, on closer inspection, proved to be personal confessions of strange poetic power and, more important, supplied the key to the tragedy of his disappearance. With the harshness and concision of roughly fashioned wood-cuts, the anonymous poet—thus we must designate him, a true poet of the people—lays down his passionate confession. In a heightened narrative the youth's irresistible temptation by a gipsy-girl is related, his inner struggle and self-defence, eventual defeat and anguish of conscience. Having broken the laws of his ancestors, he is now driven from the paternal soil by the knowledge of his guilt. All this is told with a simplicity and imaginative strength, with a depth of inborn feeling and a delicacy in ethical matters which breathe the spirit of true folk song. It was to be expected that Janáček's artistic imagination should be fired by these homely and heartfelt outpourings of an afflicted heart; this is an aspect of the *Jenufa*-world, and, moreover, a good deal of the pantheistic experience of Nature found in *The Cunning Little Vixen*.

These twenty-two songs are masterly musical miniatures. Janáček set the poems of the lost peasant-lad with marvellous economy. Everything is reduced to spare, expressive formulae, without any superfluous adornments—the latter, indeed, were always avoided by Janáček. Emotion and intellect are perfectly balanced and coalesce in a richly pointed musical idiom that rivets the attention of the listener.

Nature is frequently depicted: the play of the glow-worms in the nocturnal forest (No. 3), the twittering of the swallows (No. 4), summer afternoon and the flight of the magpie (No. 19), the heavy tread of the oxen (Nos. 5 and 6). For Janáček, these are the counterpoints of Nature to the human drama, mysteriously interwoven with, and participating in, the latter. Thus, the hovering, alluring motif of the dancing glow-worms forms the musical and emotional background to the glittering enticement of the gipsy who ensnares the boy with 'two glowing eyes'. Similarly, the heavy tread of the ploughing oxen in the Moussorgskian fifth and sixth songs becomes an image of the boy's heaviness of heart. The descriptive musical stylisation of characteristic poetic motives is quite in agreement with the practices of romantic song-writing—cf. Nos. 3, 5, 6, 8, 11, 14, 19; albeit on the level of Janáček's realism which is allied organically to the unadorned immediacy of the texts.

The melodic invention is entirely in the spirit of Eastern Moravian folk song; we find the typical terse two-bar phrases, the frequent bar-changes, the derivation of declamation from verbal accents, free modulation in accordance with the degree of inner tension, modal colouring. We have already commented (cp. Ch. 9, p. 99) on the frequent occurrence, especially in these songs, of a stereotyped melodic motif consisting of the combination of a second with a subsequent third or fourth. Numbers in which declamation predominates alternate with lyrical pieces of strange, melancholy beauty, with indeterminate changes between

major and minor, occasional modal touches and broadly conceived highly emotional melodies. One such melody is the
marvellous eighth song, 'Look Not, Ye Oxen . . .'; another the
fourteenth song, 'The Sun has Risen . . .'. One of the most
personal inspirations of Janáček is the seductive, yet somehow
doom-laden, melodic phrase, 'Be welcome, Jan . . .' with which
the gipsy greets her suitor in the ninth song. But the cosmopolitan
idiom, too, so characteristic of this creative period, finds its
place here. Thus in the emphatic whole-tone melody of the
second song ('Is she still here, that gipsy . . .') Janáček reveals his
strong inclination towards impressionism so typical in this Diary
(Nos. 2, 3, 10) and altogether frequent whenever his music
depicts the moods of Nature (*The Cunning Little Vixen*). The
accompaniment figures, on the other hand, which are derived
from the technique of the czimbalon—primal musical impulses,
as it were, surrounding a main note by arabesque figurations
(Nos. 10, 13, 17) or by glissando-like passages (No. 16)—point
again at Janáček's folkloristic roots. How iridescent and seductive
is his tone, the atmosphere created by the music, in the song of the
gipsy when she praises the freedom of nomadic life, how mysteriously does this alto-solo combine with the floating chords for
three women's voices in which the forest and all Nature seem to
raise their voice, accompanying the human drama as a soulful
echo.

The gay *Nursery Rhymes* (*Rikadla*, 1925) owe their existence
both to Janáček's bent for the capricious, as also to the continuation of the free and easy mood in which he wrote the wind-
sextet *Youth*. Witty and pointed, they stem from the sphere of
Russian children's songs, and particularly those of Moussorgsky.
Angular as puppets, at times a little pensive, mostly, however, brisk
and ebullient, of vivid musical characterisation (which is obviously
inspired by the funny drawings of Láda, Sekora and Hala), full
of a quizzical recognition of the grotesque and absurd, these

eighteen impromptus flash past the listener. Originally set for three women's voices with piano and clarinet, the *Nursery Rhymes* were enlarged by the composer in 1927 and rewritten for two sopranos, two altos, three tenors, two basses, piano, two clarinets, piccolo, two flutes, two bassoons, double-bassoon, double-bass, ocarina and toy-drum.

This is the place to mention Janáček's arrangements of folk songs of which there are several edited collections, including *Folk Poetry of Hukvaldy* (*Ukvalská lidová poesie v písních*, 1898), *Garland of Moravian Folk Songs* (*Kytice s národních písní moravských*, 1890), *Twenty-six Folk Ballads* (*26 balad lidových*, 1906-16), *Folk Songs for Voice and Piano* (*Lidové písně pro zpěv a klavír*, undated), *Folk Songs of Moravia* (*Moravské lidové písně*, 1922), and the charming *Songs of Silesia* (*Slezské písně*, 1918). The master approached these settings with his usual sensitive respect for the musical vernacular of his homeland. The accompaniments are reduced to a minimum (excepting the colourful czimbalon chord-figurations of some of the Hukvaldy Songs), and the melodic and rhythmic freedom of the tunes remains untrammelled. Two-part singing in thirds—called *Notturno* by Janáček, as these sensuous, extended tunes are usually sung in the evening—is noted down by the composer in some settings, as for instance in the *Twenty-six Folk Ballads*.

After he left the Old Brno St. Augustine's Abbey, Janáček's artistic interest in church music had gradually declined. The popular, sentimentalising conventions of the nineteenth century (Schiedermeier and others) were as unlikely to satisfy his strongly individual vision as the bloodless 'authentic' Cecilian tradition on which his schooling in sacred music was based. His subsequent sporadic contributions to this genre are, therefore, either occasional academic works, written for teaching purposes at the organ-school (such as the fragment of a *Mass* in E flat, 1907/8, consisting of Kyrie, Credo and Agnus), or else excursions of his mature style into the religious sphere that are entirely at variance with the traditional church music, such as the *Offertorium Constitues* for male chorus and organ (1903) or the *Ave Maria* (*Zdrávas Maria*, probably of the same year) for tenor solo, mixed chorus, violin and organ. In the early gradual *Exaudi Deus* (1877) for mixed chorus and the *Ten Czech Church Songs* (*Deset českých cirkevních zpěvů*, 1881), which are harmonisations of existing Czech church melodies, the influence of Bach's chorale harmonisations is apparent, albeit with a strong Slavonic flavour.

It was not until his two oratorios *Amarus* and *The Eternal Gospel* (Věčné evangelium), and above all, his *Glagolitic Mass*, that Janáček found congenial religious subjects that enabled him to speak his own musical language. *Amarus* (1897), for three solo voices, mixed chorus and orchestra, is to some extent a self-confession: his longing for happiness and joy in life inspired him to write this full-blooded, warm-hearted work. The text by Jaroslav Vrchlický must have moved the former abbey-scholar Janáček in more ways than one. The monk Amarus, a love-child, has the task in his abbey of tending the light before the image of the Mother of God. In his meditations, it is revealed to him that if he should ever fail to replenish the oil of the altar-light he would meet his death. Spring arrives, and in his yearning for life and love, Amarus follows a couple of lovers into the world of young blossoms. He forgets the light, and the monks find his body by the grave of his mother.

This work is contemporary with *Jenufa*, and has therefore many stylistic similarities with this early master-piece; on the other hand, the oratorical pathos of the funeral-scene in *Šárka* (Act III) finds an echo in the epilogue of *Amarus*. In common with *Jenufa*, *Amarus* has typical text and word repetitions, usually enhanced emotionally by an extension of the melodic intervals ('. . . that is the reward of his sin,' pp. 3–4; 'Say, when shall I perish . . .' p. 12, etc.); the dark-toned chorus '. . . was upright and sad,'

(p. 6), too, is reminiscent of that opera. The technique of associative motifs, so characteristic of Janáček's operas, is used here, too, though tentatively; thus, when the modal opening theme (clarinets, celli) returns in varied form, as at the words 'was upright and sad,' (p. 6), '. . . hardly had he spoken these words,' (p.13) and as an accompaniment to the chorus (pp. 16–17). Another important melodic character of the prelude, the energetic modal theme of the violas and horns, reappears again in the funeral march of the epilogue (p. 46). In the spring scene (pp. 24–36) the dramatic pulse quickens. Janáček, true dramatist that he is, enhances the music's expressiveness; descriptive details are woven into the musical texture, and choral interjections create a magical mood. The atmosphere of this scene, fraught with an unalterable fate, is like an anticipation of The Diary of a Young Man who Vanished. Amarus was first performed in December 1900, under the direction of Ferdinand Vach in the Moravian county-town of Kroměříž.

The Eternal Gospel, too, is based on a poetic subject by Jaroslav Vrchlický; in this case a subject of well-nigh unearthly idealism. The work comes from the time of his struggle for Jenufa, that creatively rather barren period in Janáček's life during which his powers grew towards the great operas and instrumental works of the twenties. It is interesting that Janáček, the realist and psychologist, should embrace a text of such unreal, lyrical-contemplative quality as that of The Eternal Gospel. Was it done from a desire to find a counterpart to his realistic art in the sphere of religious idealism? In any case, it is certain that the theme of eternal evangelical love encompassing mankind was a close emotional and philosophical concern of Janáček; it was a preparation, as it were, for the grand fresco of human misery and eventual redemption which he was to create at the end of his life in The House of the Dead.

The Eternal Gospel (1914) is written for two solo voices—

soprano and tenor—chorus and orchestra; the first performance took place in February 1917 at Prague under the direction of Jaroslav Křička. The vision of the eternal gospel is described in four parts: in the first, the rise of the 'great morn' (Tempo di marcia); in the second, the appearance of the angel; in the third the annunciation of the glad tidings:

> The Kingdom of the Father was the starry dome,
>
> The Kingdom of the Son the happy smiling sun,
>
> The Kingdom of the Spirit shall be the eternal light.
>
> Both Kingdoms have perished,
>
> But the third will last for ever . . .

The fourth part closes with the glad tidings of eternal love.

Musically, the work is again based on Janáček's technique of associative motifs, with interesting melodic combinations resulting, such as in the second half of the third part at the prophecy of the new kingdom. *The Eternal Gospel* is a work of pure, ideal faith, but musically not one of the representative works of the Moravian master.

The cantata *Na Soláni čarták* is of the same period (1911). This is the name of an inn, situated in the eastern mountains of Moravia near the Slovakian border, that was frequented by smugglers and frontier guards. The text by M. Kurt (Max Kunert) tells of the love between the innkeeper's daughter and an unknown stranger. The music of passion is interwoven with gay, popular dance strains. The social responsibility frequently expressed here secures for the work a modest place in the series of socially-minded choral compositions by Janáček. The cantata is scored for male chorus and orchestra. Its first performance took place at Prostějov, in 1912.

Janáček's creative powers, far from losing anything of their original vitality with increasing age, in fact gained in sublime concentration, clarity and expressive force. It was this unusual phenomenon that enabled the master at an advanced age to write one of his most fiery and vital works, the *Glagolitic Mass* of 1926. This is a unique, inimitable work, in artistic outlook as well as in style, and although it is a setting of the Ordinary of the Mass, the *Glagolitic Mass* can scarcely be considered a piece of church music in the liturgical sense.

As with many works of Janáček, the plan of the Mass and the circumstances of its composition were rather unusual. The text, a vernacular version of the Latin *ordinarium missae*, was taken by the composer from an ecclesiastical periodical, and the Old-Slavonic language of the time of St. Cyril and St. Method (9th century) in which the traditional prayers were cast, was mistakenly called 'glagolitic' by him—a name that refers only to the Old-Slavonic script and the Old-Slavonic, pre-cyrillic alphabet (consisting of Greek and Eastern characters), but not to the language itself. As the music is composed in accordance with modern Czech accentuation, it often disagrees with the scansion of Old-Slavonic, whose semi-vowels and nasals are ignored by Janáček. The setting is, however, quite congruent with the existing popular text; moreover, the Latin *ordinarium* can easily be substituted.

Although the *Glagolitic Mass* accepts some conventions of traditional mass-writing, its basic character is quite out of the ordinary. There is in this Mass no humble adoration, no mystical search of the individual for God; the work is an exuberant hymn to life, a breath-taking affirmation of the bond between the creator and mankind. Here, Janáček has scaled the highest rungs of his pantheistic faith; here he talks to his creator on terms of equality—not out of blasphemous arrogance, but out of profound confidence in Him, and a sense of being part in the essence of the godhead. The fact that Janáček was thinking of a service under the open sky underlines further the elemental character of this work.

In its formal structure, the *Glagolitic Mass* follows Janáček's dynamic variation principle. From the fanfare-motif of the Introduction,

Example 40, 2 bars

the main idea of the Kyrie arises, and so, freely transformed, does that of the Gloria as well (cp. Ch. 9, p. 100); this is a typical example of Janáček's linear primitivism, and of his way of developing extended movements from a basic melodic formula. In the Credo, the Kyrie motif is inserted, virtually unchanged, into the closing cadence of the opening phrase; by way of a free thematic metamorphosis, the Sanctus, with its orchestral melody reminiscent of Smetana, is linked to the Agnus Dei.

Example 41, a) Sanctus opening.
              b) Sanctus p. 67.
              c) Agnus opening.

The sound of kettle-drums and brass, characteristic of Janáček (*Sinfonietta*), lends the hieratic opening fanfares a barbaric splendour. The choral Kyrie is followed by the soprano solo of the Christe Eleison whose accompaniment figure is a free inversion of the Kyrie motif. The Kyrie ends with a passionate outcry, carried by harsh harmonies. We have already mentioned (cp. Ch. 9, p. 100 and Ch. 10, p. 113) the grandly conceived, bell-like melody of the Gloria. At the words 'And peace on earth', (p. 14) we find an interesting anticipation of the Sanctus melody with its wide interval steps. Further features of the movement are the acceleration of the bell-figure in the Allegro middle-part, the vocal passages in thirds (' Thou that takest away the sins of the world'), the orgiastic 'Amen' (cp. Ch. 10, p. 121). The sombre harshly declamatory opening theme of the Credo forms, like a ritornel, one of the driving melodic impulses of the movement (cp. Ch. 9, p. 100). Instead of the traditional, mystical '*Et incarnatus est*', Janáček offers a dramatic vision of Christ's descent from Heaven—almost a fall from Heaven ('He was incarnated'). There follows an orchestral interlude which may refer to scenes from the life of the Saviour: Andante—Jesus praying in the desert; *un poco più mosso*—Jesus blessing the people; Allegro (organ solo)—the passion. The cruel realism of the Crucifixus, despite its Stravinskyan harmonies, does not differ in essentials from Bach's conception in the *St. John* and *St. Matthew Passion*. The wild outcry of 'was crucified' and the hammer-blows of the chorus form the climax of the movement. The beginning of the final section 'I believe . . .' is not devoid of operatic traits.

Above a gently undulating, ostinato-like orchestral melody (cp. Example 41a), the four solo voices enter with their threefold 'Holy'—solemnly and authoritatively, without the humble submissiveness of traditional Sanctus movements. The orchestral theme surrounds the vigorous vocal phrase like a gentle halo. At the words 'Heaven and Earth are full of Thy glory', the tempo becomes livelier, the ostinato changes into a frolicking, jubilant counterpoint to the voices, and the worldly gaiety of the passage is underscored by operatic turns ('Blessed is he that cometh . . .'). The lyrical, inward Agnus Dei leads into the agitated organ solo, a fantasy on a two-bar ostinato theme, and the barbaric-solemn Intrada with which the work ends. Perhaps the idea behind an Intrada introduced at such an unusual place is the processional return of the faithful to the church after the open-air service. In any case, this again is Janáček's individual way of stepping before his creator. 'I want to show people how to talk to God' was his comment on the Mass. At the first performance in Brno, on December 5th, 1927, this Dionysiac-Christian outburst shook the world of music.

CHAPTER 13

ORCHESTRAL WORKS

Whilst in his own country Janáček is appreciated chiefly as a vocal composer—the creator of choruses, the Glagolitic Mass and, above all, of operas—his international fame seems largely founded on his instrumental works. This is but natural if one considers the difficulties that are met in translating the texts of a vocal music that is strongly national in attitude. In Janáček's case, there is an added difficulty arising from his individual manner of composing which, as we know, was closely connected with the vernacular and the folklore of his country. The fact that some of his orchestral works could maintain their place by the side of the great popular operas, and were, indeed, preferred to the latter by some musicians, is surely a certain criterion of their artistic value. Yet in spite of this, Janáček's instrumental music is often considered second-rate—in comparison with his most important operas—an offshoot, as it were, of his linguistically conceived vocal works.

The problematical point of Janáček's orchestral style is easily perceived: as soon as his fragmentary idiom had to subsist without the aid of a text, there was bound to set in a certain poverty and shortwindedness of the thematic structure. But Janáček has met this danger half-way. The emotional and poetical foundation given to him by language is supplied in his instrumental compositions by their various programmatic contents; these give sufficient impetus to his invention and at the same time guarantee a modicum of formal logic. However, Janáček was perfectly able to compose—on a purely musical plane, so to speak—without these stimuli, as is shown by such masterpieces as the *Sinfonietta* or the *Concertino*. In situations where lesser composers would undoubtedly have foundered, he succeeded, thanks to the dynamic vitality of his ideas, in creating living forms, if only in the category of the miniature. The disparity between his vocal and instrumental *oeuvre* is, in fact, only a quantitative one; it seems that in certain phases of his development he was intent on applying to the instrumental sphere the experiences he had made in the realm of vocal music.

Janáček's early instrumental works are completely under the sway of the classical conservatism of his youth; his choice of precisely defined formal modals expresses this very well. To this group belong the *Suite for String Orchestra*, the *Idyll* for string orchestra, the *Lachian Dances* and the *Suite for Orchestra*, op. 3.

The *Suite for String Orchestra* (1877) and the *Idyll* (1878) are in many respects still very uncertain attempts at simple forms. In the first movement of the *Suite*, an energetic opening theme gives rise to a broadly conceived melody (Moderato, G minor) which attains its full emotional development in the second part of the movement. Neither here nor in the subsequent movements do the titles that are taken over from the baroque suite agree with the character of the movements. The second movement (Allemande), an Adagio cantabile of noble lyrical pathos and ample modulations, has nothing in common with the traditional form of this name. The third movement (Sarabande), with its even time, upholding a conventionally harmonised, slow-stepping melody, is irregular too. The fourth movement, a Scherzo with a sharply rhythmicised theme and a calm Trio, conforms most closely to type; Janáček it seems, had no scruples in incorporating this piece in a historical form. The fifth movement (Air) has a contemplative melody with subtle contrasts between the high and low ranges of the strings. The sixth movement, Finale, is in a ternary mould approaching sonata-form. Despite its melodic charm, the work is uneven, formally inelastic and immature. Together with late-romantic *clichés* of melody and harmony, we find the strong influence of Dvořák.

The *Idyll* is a similar case. This work, too, is conceived as a suite, but the movements are planned on an ampler scale, mostly ternary—with the exception of the sonata-like fourth and rondo-like seventh movement—and in technical execution more mature and craftsmanlike than the preceding *Suite*. The work's fresh melodies reflect the holiday mood of the composer—the work was sketched during his visit to Oettingen in Bavaria. The influence of Dvořák is paramount; popular dance elements are frequently encountered (second movement, middle part of the fifth movement, sixth movement); late-romantic and historising trends have almost entirely disappeared; at several points, however, Janáček's individual style breaks through, as for instance in the ostinate-like 5/4 motion of the third movement (Cp. Ch. 10, p. 106), or in the lyrical pathos of the fifth movement (Adagio) whose *Dumka* character, deriving from Dvořák, has been fully assimilated and individualised by Janáček. The work consisted at first of six movements (with the conventional Scherzo as a Finale) but was subsequently extended to seven movements. In its foursquare main subject, the new final movement is reminiscent of the character of the baroque suite; special mention must be made of the asymmetrical periodisation of the second subject (B major).

The main work among these early orchestral compositions are the *Lachian Dances* (1889-90). In the picturesque language of the preface to the present version of these dances (1928), Janáček conjures up the atmosphere of his Lachian home district. 'In the valley, below the castle of Hukvaldy, there stood the inn 'u Harabašů'—a flying stone could have thrown it over . . . Inside, smoke and fug, one could have cut the air, Žofka Harabašová, the dancer, glides from one partner to the next. That was forty-five years ago. The marvellous landscape, the quiet people, their language as soft as if one were cutting butter . . .'

The *Lachian Dances* are the first fully matured orchestral work of Janáček and at the same time his first printed composition, published as op. 2. They are arrangements of traditional dance-tunes from the district of Lachia and Vallachia (Lašsko and Valašsko), two folkloristically identical regions of his Eastern Moravian homeland. Considered as a result of Janáček's folk-loristic studies, they belong to the same category as Dvořák's *Slavonic Dances*; Janáček's settings are, however, less stylised than Dvořák's, and the original character of the dances is more faithfully preserved.

The existing six dances have originated from the third volume (*Vallachian Dances*, Valašské tance) of Janáček's *National Dances of Moravia* (Národuí tance na Moravě)[1] arranged for piano duet and piano solo. They form a suite of pieces of contrasting character and expression. First comes a leisurely Andante dance in 3/4 time; actually, a combination of two slow dances with a fast postlude. This 'Old-time dance' ('Starodávný') is usually called 'Dance with the kerchief' or 'Dance with the staff', because there is in it one supernumerary dancer who swings a staff decorated with many-coloured ribbons until he is joined by a partner. The second piece is a moderately animated Allegretto movement in 3/4 time (Požehnání). Its eight-bar ritornello-like theme undergoes the development of a rondo episode without, however, acquiring a contrasting second subject. The Dymák (third movement) is a very rhythmical dance of great latent

[1] A selection of *Hannakian Dances* (Hanácke tance) of the same collection, combined with the Vallachian Dances, forms the basis of the ballet *Rákoct Rákoczy* (1891).

energy, which during the course of the piece breaks out in a Prestissimo section, only to subside again towards the end. The piece is in rondo form. There follows another 'Old-time dance' (fourth movement); with its polonaise-like main subject and its tonality suspended between major and minor, this is full of poetic charm. The brisk Čeladenský (fifth movement) is similar in character and structure to the quick Dymák. The Finale (sixth movement) is a popular dance in ternary form, Pílky, like a polka in character—the brilliant popular highlight of the *Lachian Dances*.

The *Hannakian Dances*,[1] which sprang from the same source as the *Lachian Dances*, are as yet unpublished and therefore not accessible to the author. They exist in an orchestral version as well as in an arrangement for piano–duet. Some numbers have been used in the ballet *Rákoct Rákoczy*.

The next considerable work of this early period is the *Orchestral Suite*, op. 3 (1891), known also under its first title of *Serenade*. In this four-movement work, Janáček seeks to give symphonic stylisation to vernacular forms and melody-types, thus investing them—in comparison with the *Lachian Dances*—with a weightier meaning and placing them within a wider formal frame. Generally speaking, this attempt was not successful; one could even say that here Janáček sacrificed his usual spontaneity and popular freshness of invention to his higher artistic ambitions. The suite begins (first movement) in the manner of a prelude with a romantically solemn theme which later returns in a faster version and is relieved by a cantabile melody. The second movement, Adagio, points towards Dvořákian and neo-romantic models. In the third movement, Janáček has gone back to the dance Požehnání of the *Lachian Dances*. The original plan is formally expanded here and harmonically simplified, with the

[1]The Hanna is a fertile plain along the river Morava in the environs of the Moravian town Olomouc.

result that the movement has lost much of its erstwhile charm. The Finale of the suite has the character of a sparkling toccata in simple rondo form. From the same year of 1891 comes an unpublished *Adagio* for large orchestra, a composition of no great significance.

During the following twenty years, Janáček composed nothing for orchestra, with the exception of small occasional pieces.[1] During those years his creative powers were absorbed in his vocal works, particularly the operas. Not before 1912 did he return to orchestral music. His matured humanity, his Czech patriotism, stimulated by the experiences of the first world war, and his new, purified attitude towards the symphonic poem, enabled him to write three works of this kind during the next eight years (1912-1920): *The Fiddler's Child* (*Šumařovo dítě*, 1912), *Taras Bulba* (1915-1918) and the *Ballad of the Blaník* (*Ballada Blanícká*, 1920).

The orchestral ballad in one movement, *The Fiddler's Child*, is inspired by Svatopluk Čech's poem of the same name. The old fiddler has died; he has left nothing but his fiddle and the child in the cradle. Now, the nanny who nurses the child dreams that the fiddler has returned to this world; she sees him standing like a shadow next to the cradle, playing a sweet, bewitching song whose strains remove the child from earthly misery to a blissful beyond. In the morning, the village-eldest finds the child dead in his cradle, but the fiddle has vanished.

Janáček has divided this romantic poem musically into three parts: the sad life of the minstrel and his death (bars 1–194); his ghostly appearance (bars 194–424), and the finding of the child's body (bars 425–483). The three sections are connected thematically; according to the changes of mood and the images of the

[1] e.g. an orchestral arrangement of the Russian folk dance *Kozáček* by Nik. Vevericov (1899), or a setting of the Serbian round-dance Kolo for orchestra (1899). The original version of the overture to *Jenufa* was published in 1906 as an independent orchestral piece under the title *Jealousy* (*Žarlivost*).

text, however, further musical sub-sections have been created within this framework whose rondo-like arrangement strengthens the work's structural unity. The two main themes of the ballad appear in the first few bars: the melancholy and harmonically vague opening theme, played in octaves by the flutes—in its subsequent transformations it is revealed as an expression of 'evil', of the harshness and cruelty of daily life (bars 151, 166, 425, etc.)—and the dreamy melody of the fiddler, in which the plaintive tone of the East Slavonic Dumka vibrates (cp. Ch. 10, p. 107). This melody is entrusted to a solo violin and also appears in the most diversified forms: first passionately, with the introductory step of a fourth enlarged to an octave or a tenth (bar 338), then ghostly in C flat major, pp, in high position (bar 364), lastly invested with a scherzo-like character (bars 74 and 87). These main ideas are joined by some secondary themes; thus the elegiac melody (bar 12), stated by the violins and contrapuntally connected with the fiddler's theme, which, according to Janáček's words, is to express 'the soul of those people who lead a harsh life in the poor shepherd's huts of our villages', or the brief, folk song-like Adagio idea in C sharp minor (bar 119), or the three-note motif of the whimpering child, subsequently expounded into an expressive melody for the solo oboe (bar 289).

Altogether, the programmatic employment of individual solo instruments is characteristic of this work: the solo violin of the fiddler, the oboe of the suffering child; at a certain point a solo bassoon brings (bar 227) the menacing first theme; the melody of the poor shepherd people is given to the divided violins, etc. All the same, the orchestration is in many places uneven or overloaded, particularly where an excess of figurative accompaniment formulae threatens the melodic and textural equilibrium (bars 87, 417, etc.).

In its spirit, *The Fiddler's Child* is an expression of Janáček's philosophy of compassion and his faith in a redemption and beatification beyond all the misery of this world. This symphonic poem inhabits, therefore, the same spiritual sphere as *Jenufa*, *Maryčka Magdonová*, and *The House of the Dead*.

During the first world war, when the hope for national independence roused the Czech people to ardent patriotic enthusiasm, Janáček's symphonic rhapsody *Taras Bulba* came into being (1915-18). The work is the composer's contribution to the national fighting spirit, and beyond this, a token of his Russophilia; a strong Russia was to him a guarantee for the renascence of a powerful Slav culture. Characteristically, *Taras Bulba* was subsequently dedicated to the 'Czech armed forces', that is to the army of the newly founded national state.

Among all the grim figures of the Slavonic past, that of the Ukrainian Cossack leader Taras Bulba is one of the most gloomy and tragic. From Gogol's well-known story, Janáček selected three significant episodes whose basic theme are heroic patriotism and self-negation. Engaged in the fight against the Poles, Taras Bulba kills his younger son Andrij who has betrayed the national cause because of his love for the daughter of the enemy leader (first movement). Captured by the enemy, his elder son Ostap awaits his public execution. In order to comfort him, Taras mingles with the crowd of the spectators, and as he makes himself known to his son, he forfeits his own life (second movement). Taras, condemned to death at the stake, proclaims in a prophetic vision the imminent triumph of his people (third movement). This subject which hardly affords any light relief, has been worked into a symphonic triptych by Janáček, and thanks to his dramatic pictorial skill, there are moments of strong impact in his music.

In the first part, 'The Death of Andrij', two spheres of emotion confront each other: that of duty, victorious over the bonds of blood, which makes the father the executioner of his erring son, and that of the loving youth's warm humanity. The melancholy opening melody (cp. Ch. 10, p. 120), which is to return during the course of the movement in the most divers musical and emotional guise, belongs to the world of the protagonist, Taras Bulba. When the loving father grows into the judicial leader of the people, this melody (dolce, con dolore) changes into a harsh, commanding gesture (bars 200–228), and retains its dramatic impetus (bars 229–240). Being an experienced musical dramatist, Janáček knows the means by which to preserve the symphonic unity of diverse parts; thus, the melody of Taras, freely transformed into a semiquaver figure—in Janáček's typical style of variations which also includes here an alteration of the original intervals—appears again in the second and third movements (bars 192 and 159 respectively) as a sort of associative motif. The father-son relation is indicated in the first movement by the contrapuntal combination of the same motif—in inversion —with a vehement (più mosso) passage in the woodwinds (bars 19–23, 31–34, 43–46). Andrij, the lover, has been graced by Janáček with one of the most touching and tender love melodies since Tchaikovsky (bars 100–199, 259–270). Played by a solo oboe, this carries an element of warmth and soft dreaminess into the otherwise sombre colours and moods of the score. The programmatic grouping of these main subjects results in a free rondo form.

The second movement 'The Death of Ostapov' is of a smaller cast. This is musically more simple and structurally more concise than the first movement. An abrupt motif of fourths forms a sort of ritornello which is used melodically as well as in the form of an ostinato figure (bars 71–109), and lends the piece its urgent vigour. It is joined by a chromatically inflected theme of dragging rhythm (bars 11–55, 64–70, 110–170 with interruptions), and by a third idea, a popular, lyrical motif (bars 73–109), mostly harmonised in sixths.

The third movement, too, 'The Prophecy and Death of Taras Bulba', has a rondo-like form. A brooding tune in the bassoons, accompanied by the cellos, opens the piece, and returns in melodic augmentation in the violins (bars 44–51). In a subsequent episode, a variant of the commanding Taras motif from the first movement appears and leads to a great outburst (bars 87–128) that is followed, by way of recapitulation, by the first subject of the movement and a further quotation of the Taras motif (bar 159). The extensive coda is intended as the poetical and musical climax of the work, the prophecy of Taras Bulba (bars 166–190), and leads to a hymn-like section with organ and accompanying bells (bars 191–230).

In *Taras Bulba*, Janáček has employed the orchestral resources of late romanticism in grand style. Nowhere else is his orchestral apparatus as ample or his mixtures of colour as variegated as here. The orchestration consisting of triple woodwind (piccolo, cor anglais and double bassoon are added to the traditional double woodwind), four horns, three trumpets, three trombones and tuba, harp, bells, percussion (including triangle and tambourine) and organ lends the work density and power of sound; this, however, is not always used to the best advantage by the composer, particularly in the third part. Solo passages are again employed to great poetical effect—the melody of Taras, played by the cor anglais, the organ solos, Andrij's love-tune on the oboe, etc.

The third work in the series of Janáček's symphonic poems is *The Ballad of the Blaník* (*Ballada Blanícká*, 1920). The legendary mountain within which slumber the heroes who are some day to gain the nation its freedom, is a favourite subject of Czech mythology (cp. Smetana's symphonic poem *Blaník*). In the poetic version of Jaroslav Vrchlický used by Janáček, however, the warriors change into workers, their swords and arms become ploughs, scythes and sickles—thus, the pious Jira finds the knights assembled on Good Friday, the day of the year on which the mountain opens up for a while. Coming after the tragic-heroic vision of *Taras Bulba*, this subject expressed Janáček's allegiance to the spirit of construction and peaceful activity in the new Czechoslovak state.

The fundamental tenor of the composition is one of idyllic, solemn optimism. The formal plan is again rondo-like, and based on four main ideas. The first subject, an undulating, meandering idea in A flat minor, is subjected to manifold variation; so is the related second melodic idea (bars 10–12). Its intervals enlarged and its rhythm accelerated, the former theme gains in expressiveness until it becomes a jagged shape which may perhaps stand for the Blaník mountain (bars 224, 273); the latter theme recurs during the course of the piece mainly in tonal and rhythmic variation (bars 46, 76, 97, 159). A calm, slow-moving chorale in modal colouring (bars 41, 187), followed by a hymn-like melody (A flat major) in the horns and harps (bars 54, 178, 215, 267, 269) represent the religious aspect of the Blaník legend.

The music of this symphonic poem is pale and less spontaneous as compared with the preceding works. The element of contrast, one of Janáček's most effective devices, is here reduced to a minimum; rhythmically, too, the piece is calmer and rather uniform, and, therefore, compared with Janáček's other music, the poorer for it. The same criticism can be made of the orchestration; the customary solo passages are totally absent here.

With the *Sinfonietta* (1926), Janáček reached the zenith of his orchestral works. Nowhere is his instrumental idiom as sovereign, free, self-assured and worldly-wise; and yet it does not lose its national accents. Although he remains faithful to his characteristic idiom, his style is of a thematic density and formal conciseness as in no other work. His inspiration has freed itself from its habitual literary and extra-musical stimulus, and has created a series of five orchestral miniatures that are of absolute mastery in invention, sound and structure.

The *Sinfonietta* owes its existence to a mass rally of the national sports movement, Sokol, in Prague. For this occasion, Janáček had composed a fanfare for brass which he subsequently enlarged to the divertimento form of the *Sinfonietta* by adding the remaining movements. The first movement and the close of the Finale are based on the original fanfare.

A seven-bar idea of asymmetrical periodisation, written for thirteen brass instruments and kettle-drums, opens the fanfare of the first movement. Over the slow-moving fifths of the tubas in the bass are placed the short, concise melodic periods of the trumpets that lead via seven variations to a brilliant final apotheosis—in its simplicity and naturalness, this is an inimitable flash of genius. The theme, conceived in an aeolian E flat minor, is notated without key-signature. The second movement (Andante) begins with a rotating demi-semiquaver figure on the clarinets, with which a brief, syncopated motif (trombones, bassoons) is combined. Later (bar 31) a lyrical melody detaches itself from the rotating figure—an augmentation of the former motif, accompanied by its original form. In a further episode (bars 61–70), the melody appears once more, in A flat minor and in rhythmic variation; lastly, its melodic inversion, blown by the trumpets, comes to the fore (bars 129–139). The main subject of the movement (bar 5) is a lively dance tune (cp. Ch. 9, p. 97) which, after a broad exposition subsequently returns and rounds off the movement by way of a coda. A short, humorous episode (bars 55–60) is melodically reminiscent of Dvořák. The noble pathos of the third movement's (Moderato) main subject places this piece within the series of melancholy ballads which, even more than other conventions, forms an important link connecting Janáček with Eastern Slavonic music. The dumka-like melody, first stated by the strings, comes forward repeatedly in the manner of a rondo theme, and is relieved by two lively episodes (bars 39–75, formed out of the original accompanying figure of the subject, and bars 81–172, including the Moussorgsky-like section, bars

146–172). The fourth movement (Allegretto), too, with its modal polka theme (lydian D flat major) that is developed into an ostinato, underlines Janáček's affinity with Eastern Moravian folk music (cp. Ch. 9, p. 98). The melody is developed in variation form and appears in varied instrumental combinations, occasionally enlivened by humorous counterpoints. In its impetuous vitality, this movement is a highlight of the *Sinfonietta*. The Finale (Andante con moto) begins with a popular melody in the flutes, accompanied by lively triplet-figuration in the strings. In the course of the movement, the elegiac character of the theme is enhanced; it is played alternately by a solo clarinet, a solo oboe and a solo flute to the accompaniment of strings. A scherzoid middle-part (bars 62–92) leads back to the repeat of the opening melody, now extended. The movement ends with the recapitulation of the fanfare, this time supported by the full orchestra and forming a powerful final climax to the work.

Vladimír Helfert has called the *Sinfonietta* Janáček's classical masterpiece. In its melodic and rhythmic breadth, its clarity of structure and kaleidoscopic orchestration, the work bears witness to Janáček's inspired skill for creating great art within a small space.

CHAPTER 14

CHAMBER MUSIC AND PIANO WORKS

As with all other branches of Janáček's *oeuvre*, his chamber music also forms a world of its own. With the exception of some vocal works, his style is nowhere as distinct and individual—and that with regard to its problematical as well as its original aspect—as in the three or four chamber music masterworks of his maturity. The miniaturistic quality of his invention is here in happy accord with the aims of a miniaturistic genre, and his individual, expressive treatment of the instruments ideally serves the personal emotionality of his style.

In matters of structure, Janáček's chamber music keeps more closely to the traditional forms than his orchestral works. Besides the frequent rondo-form we also find an occasional sonata-form. Here too, however, rhapsodical freedom of treatment is strongly in evidence, reflecting the characteristic changes of direction in Janáček's inspiration. In the concise idiom of chamber music, Janáček has uttered the deepest confessions of his soul. How often does the edifice of these forms tremble, do violent contrasts assail the structure so that one looks in vain for the homogeneousness of the ideal chamber music texture.

Janáček came to chamber music relatively late. A number of his student efforts as well as two less important works of his early maturity—the *Fairy Tale* (*Pohádka*) for Cello and piano and the *Violin Sonata*—precede the chamber music works composed in the twenties: the two string quartets, the wind-sextet *Youth* (*Mládí*), the *Concertino* and the *Capriccio*. These latter works have greatly contributed to Janáček's international reputation, in some ways more than his operas, choruses and orchestral compositions.

The chamber music works composed during his period of study at Leipzig and Vienna have for the greater part been lost, as for instance the two violin sonatas written at Leipzig and Vienna (1880), a *Minuet and Scherzo* for clarinet and piano (1880), and the string quartet composed during his Vienna Conservatoire period (1880). Of Janáček's student works, there are extant a *Romanza* for violin and piano (1879), originally belonging to a cycle of seven romanzas, and a *Dumka* for violin and piano (1880). From a later period (1908-9) came the piano trio (now lost) that was entitled 'After Tolstoy's Kreutzersonata'; its material was probably incorporated in the *First String Quartet* of 1923. To an earlier date, probably before 1913, belongs the *Ballad for Violin and Piano* which found its definite form in the *Violin Sonata* (1913-21).

The first entirely personal chamber music work of Janáček is the *Fairy Tale* (*Pohádka*, 1910, for Cello and Piano), originally entitled *The Fairy Tale of Czar Berendej*. In this three-movement work, scarce reference is made to the particular situations of the literary model;[1] it is rather the general poetical atmosphere that is reproduced in the spirit of the Eastern Slavonic folk tale (biliny). The piece is of rhapsodical character and shows an independent treatment of the two instruments. The piano part is distinguished by a marked euphony, underlined by the stereotyped patterns of semiquaver and demi-semiquaver figuration. Tempo and mood change in every movement. Melodic reminiscences from the first movement that appear towards the end of the second movement, are evidence of some programmatic intentions. The

[1] 'The Fairy Tale of Czar Berendej' by V. A. Žukovskij.

style of the *Fairy Tale*, compounded as it is of romantic and folkloristic elements, marks out this composition as an interesting intermediary link between Janáček's early style and the matured style of his years of mastery.

In the *Violin Sonata*, the glowingly emotional, rhapsodical chamber music style of the composer's middle period appears in full flower. The work is characterised by a marked passion and fulness of structure, particularly in the first and last movements. A first version of the *Sonata* was probably composed in 1913, followed by two later settings, the final one being the published form of 1921. The work crystallised around the above-mentioned *Ballad* which formed the third movement in the earlier versions; in the final setting the *Ballad* follows immediately after the first movement. Thematically the *Violin Sonata* closely approaches *Kátà Kabanová*, though this opera was not to be written until 1919-21. This affinity is at once apparent in the passionate first subject of the initial movement with its three-bar introduction that rises up in a twofold melodic arc. The second movement (Ballad) is in a lively tempo. Its main subject, a tune of stylised folk-character, alternates, in the manner of a rondo, with a cantabile melody. The cadenza-like extension of the first subject at the end of the movement, followed by a short reminder of the second subject in a demi-semiquaver figure of the piano, is in agreement with the rhapsodical nature of the piece. The scherzoid third movement begins with a pentatonically-inclined dance tune, followed by a lyrical theme (trio) reminiscent of the first movement of the *Fairy Tale*. The Finale is in sonata-form. Its modally conceived main subject, strongly resembling the first song of Kudrjáš in Kátà Kabanová, and its calm second subject are developed in cantabile duet-style.

An interval of almost ten years during which Janáček was busy with larger works, separates the *Violin Sonata* from his next chamber music opus, the *First String Quartet*. If the dates noted

by the composer—October 30th, 1923 to November 7th, 1923—
are to be relied on, the work would appear to have been written
within the short space of one week. One must not forget,
however, that the early (and now lost) Piano Trio,[1] inspired by
Tolstoy's novel 'Kreutzersonata' was most likely incorporated in
this quartet. This conjecture is supported by the musical character
of the quartet as well as by its similar subtitle: 'Inspired by L. N.
Tolstoy's 'Kreutzersonata'.

Janáček's late style is distinctly presaged in this work. The
melodic invention shows his strong affinity with Eastern Moravian
and, indeed, Russian folk music, which is yet wholly sublimated
to the point of an individual statement. The languishing two-bar
melody (Adagio) with which the first movement opens, almost
a motto-theme of the quartet—is suffused with this spirit. There
follows a light, skipping dance tune, which also bears a folkloristic
(Russian) stamp. The allusion to the first subject in the second
movement—disguised as a jerky scherzo theme—and the return
of this Adagio melody in the Finale where, in a different rhythmical shape, it becomes the main subject, are signs of Janáček's
intense concern with the unification and concentration of the
structure. The scherzoid second movement brings in its middle
part (bars 129–144) an interesting fusion, typical for Janáček, of
the movement's two themes—the angular main subject, and the
singable second subject. The third movement (con moto), too,
begins on folkloristic lines; its floating fairytale tone could almost
be called childlike. But after four bars, the final clause of the
theme suddenly bursts out into a refrain of fortissimo demi-
semiquavers—a wilful and elemental gesture typical of Janáček.
The Vivace middle part of the movement that is derived from
this figure, is harsh and of a gripping rhythmic impetus. The
main theme of the Finale—the Adagio melody of the first movement is transformed here into a lively, flowing tune and built up

[1] Written in 1908-9, first performed 1909.

to a tremendous emotional climax towards the end—is joined by an idea of exotic colouring (bar 5), reminiscent of the gipsy's song (No. X) in the song-cycle *Diary of a Young Man who Vanished*.[1] It is difficult to say to what extent this quartet concerns itself with Tolstoy's novel. But it can be safely stated that the story's atmosphere of passion and jealousy enveloped Janáček when writing this composition as well as the preceding piano trio.[2]

The individual treatment of the parts, the violent melodic contrasts, and above all, the primal power of the folkloristic themes—all these are here in the service of a passionate individual idiom.

Another work of self-revelation in Janáček's chamber music is the wind-suite *Youth* (*Mládí*). Composed in his seventieth year (1924), the four movements of this sextet for flute (piccolo), oboe, clarinet, horn, bassoon and bass-clarinet reflect the composer's memories of his student years at the St. Augustine Abbey in Brno (1865-74). The basic character of the work is therefore one of untroubled gaiety, giving way to high spirits on the one hand, and again to a pensive melancholy on the other.[3]

Stylistically, the wind-suite is a typical work of Janáček's late maturity. While expression remains highly flexible and variable, great stress is laid on the principle of thematic unification within a movement and thematic relationship between the movements (as, for instance, between the first and fourth movements). The melodic character of the *Sextet* is less indebted to folklore if compared with such a work as the *First String Quartet*. Janáček's

[1] The main themes of the first and fourth movements show a strong similarity to the twenty-second song of the *Diary of a Young Man who Vanished*.

[2] '... I had here in mind the pitiable woman who is maltreated, beaten and murdered, such as is described by Tolstoy in his story.' (From a letter of Janáček to Kamilla Stoesslová, 1924).

[3] A few months previously, the composer had written a march for piccolo, flute, bells, tambourine and piano. This *March of the Blue-tits* (*Pochod Modráčků*), so called after the blue uniforms of the pupils, was intended as a sketch for the wind-sextet *Youth*. The thematic material of this charming piece is largely re-employed in the third movement of the sextet.

chamber music of that period is marked by distinct cosmopolitan leanings. His familiarity with contemporary music acquired through attending the congresses of the *International Society of Contemporary Music* must surely have left its mark on his late chamber music style. There is evidence that the concerts of the wind ensemble "Société moderne des instruments à vent" had a direct influence on the composition of Janáček's wind-suite.

The first movement with its opening whole-tone melody has an idyllic charm that rises to gay exuberance in the livelier middle part. The main subject, a thrice-stated descending third, goes on to dominate, as a kind of ritornello, the whole movement which is cast in Janáček's free rondo form. The mood of the second movement is contemplative, mingled with gentle melancholy. The predominating idea of the movement, a slow-marching three-bar melody, is subjected to variation, each section being preceded by a short intermezzo which consists of the opening bar with the main theme and a lively descending scale-passage in 17/16 time (one 4/4 bar plus 1/16). In the third movement (Scherzo), the burlesque piccolo-tune of the opening is supported by the merry quaver-accompaniment of the first movement's middle part. The oboe-melody of the trio closes every time with a charmingly high-spirited demi-semiquaver melisma. The Finale appears to be a formally uncommitted paraphrase of, or complement to, the first movement—thematically as well as programmatically; it is a piece of irrepressible *joie de vivre*. Based on a variant of the first movement's main theme, it represents a good example of Janáček's manner of thematic development. We encounter melodic and rhythmic variations and transformations of the theme; the accompaniment figures, the key, the tempo change in quick succession; all is movement and spontaneous invention—and yet held together by an unassailable logic. Towards the end, the first movement's main subject is quoted literally: Janáček's technique of the associative motif was used with increasing frequency in his chamber music (in the two string quartets); evidently engendered in the first place by considerations of a programmatic nature, it eventually came to serve the composer in lending comprehensibility to his otherwise so diffuse structures.

In the following year, 1925, came the composition of the *Concertino* for piano, two violins, viola, clarinet, horn and bassoon. This work, too, has a certain experimental and cosmopolitan air; but the experiment does not always succeed. The present form of the *Concertino* is the result of numerous changes in the structure as well as in the instrumentation. The fact that Janáček originally planned not so much a chamber concerto in the strict sense of the word as a piano concerto with accompanying chamber orchestra —which is the natural character of the work—is proved by the title of the first manuscript: "Piano Concerto with accompaniment of two violins, viola, clarinet, horn and bassoon." While the *Concertino* can hardly be called chamber music according to classical definitions, neither is it plainly *concertante*. Only occasionally is the orchestra used by itself and in its entirety. The leading role is taken by the piano, which is joined by single solo instruments, mostly functioning as an accompaniment. Thus, the first movement with its harsh, quasi-exotic main subject and the subsequent grotesque valse, is a duet between piano and horn, the share of the latter consisting in short, motivic interjections. Similarly, we find in the second movement a duet between the piano and the shrill-sounding E flat clarinet. The brutal, tensely rhythmical chord-theme of the piano, which is later on overlaid by a duplet-melody of the clarinet, points to the world of Stravinsky and Bartok. In the third movement, the entire instrumental ensemble combines with the piano, though here, too, the instruments merely provide supplementary rhythm and colour (more rarely melody) without ever achieving a true chamber music ensemble. The movement begins with an energetic march-like theme which is treated like an ostinato. A flowing middle part, contributed chiefly by the piano, leads to a hammered-out piano cadenza which in turn is followed by the repeat of the main theme. The Finale comes nearest to the idea of a chamber ensemble, for the orchestra does here, in fact, take part for brief spells in the motivic discussion. A capricious subject, reminiscent of Janáček's *Nursery Rhymes*, dominates the movement which dashes on impetuously, regardless of formal logic and cogency. The *Concertino* is rich in these grotesque, not to say, bizarre, effects. The *concertante* element is in the main restricted to the cadenza-like solo passages of the piano which take an important place in every movement. What gives the work its special attraction, however, is the roughness and boldness of its invention and sound combinations. Janáček's 'primitivity' produces here, as it were, the effects of over-refinement; the *Concertino*'s spontaneity and challenge to the listener are quite irresistible.

On yet another occasion Janáček dealt with the problem of placing the piano within a chamber music combination, this time a wind ensemble. The *Capriccio*, written in 1926 for the one-armed pianist Otakar Hollmann is a study for the left hand; its necessarily thin piano writing is combined with a group of wind instruments, consisting of flute (piccolo), two trumpets, one tenor-tuba and three trombones. This list of instruments alone stamps the piece, by and large, as yet another experimental composition (the combination of four low and three high brass instruments!). More frequently than in other problematical works of the composer, his wilfulness (and perhaps technical inexperience) has here produced unplayable, or tonally unrealisable, passages which have remained uncorrected throughout the repeated revisions of the *Capriccio*. Thus, at the beginning of the third scherzo-like movement, the tuba is asked to execute widely extended interval leaps, followed by semiquaver-triplets. Even more wilful is the unrealistic passage in the Finale (bars 228–242) where the trumpet has demi-semiquaver sixtuplets which are taken up by the third trombone (bar 231), and are then to be continued by the three trombones in alternation. Sometimes the harmonies of the lower wind instruments move within the same range as the leading voice so that the latter becomes obscured, if not altogether extinguished (beginning of the third movement). In contrast to the *Concertino*, the piano has a secondary role. While it is in a leading position in the first movement—the main subject in its, as it were, didactic regularity has an étude-like touch—and in the Schumannesque Adagio opening of the second movement, the piano part is reduced subsequently to the status of an accompanying and colouristic element (runs, passages, broken chords in the third and fourth movements). The greatest part of the thematic work is with the wind; thus in the vivace section of the first movement, or in the exotic, fanciful trumpet-tune of the third movement that is quoted by the tuba in the Finale, or in the cantabile main idea of the Finale (flute).

Compared with the *Concertino* the harmonic and melodic character of the *Capriccio* is conventional, even romantic (second movement). The folkloristic element is almost totally excluded. All the same, Janáček created this work from inner conviction; it is even founded on a certain poetic-philosophical idea. The originally intended title 'Defiance' ('Vzdor') is evidence that the composer meant to express in this work the heroic acceptance of a cruel blow of fate—Otokar Hollmann had lost his right hand in the first world war.

The climax and conclusion of Janáček's chamber music *oeuvre* is reached in the *Second String Quartet* of 1928. It is his purest and deepest work of self-revelation; his passion for Kamilla Stoesslová had stimulated his creative powers to their highest pitch.[1] But more than that: never before has the identity of

[1] The quartet was written in twenty-two days, between January 29th and February 19th, 1928.

anáček the man and Janáček the artist been so complete and absolute as in this work where the personal irradiates the universal, and where Janáček's naturalistic and vernacular musical idiom is sublimated to represent the supra-national symbols of humanity itself. The vocal origin of his melodic writing becomes fully manifest here. These themes glow and shine in their folkloristic garb; now they tumble over themselves in a sudden transport of joy, or again grief; now they rise to mighty pathos. In this work Janáček no longer experiments: the *Second String Quartet* is the sum, the quintessence of his artistic growth, and at the same time the crowning token of his happiness and fulfilment as a man.

There should be no doubt about the intimate character of the quartet. Proud and self-assured, the seventy-four-years old composer wrote down his passionate confession, and thus he committed it to the public under the title of 'Intimate Letters'. The string quartet here becomes to him the ideal medium for his most private communications. The main subject of the first movement with its floating rubato rhythm appears as the leading motto-theme, the *idée fixe* of the work. We hear it at the end of the second movement where it is joined contrapuntally to the presto melody of the middle part (bars 181–210); we hear it in the course of the Finale in melodic and rhythmic variation (bars 194–230); nor will the sensitive listener fail to perceive the similarity between the marvellous love song in the third movement's middle part and the main subject. Janáček subsequently renounced his original intention of having the viola part taken by a viola d'amore; the part is now given to a modern viola. It has frequently to be played '*sul ponticello*' ('on the bridge') in order to achieve the gentle, nasal, vibrating sound of the viola d'amore. The second subject of the first movement is already played '*sul ponticello*'; it returns later in manifold guises. The movement closes forebodingly with the main subject, grandiose and elevated

(Grave). The first movement's free rondo form is followed by an Adagio—second movement—written on the variation principle; the lilting melody is first sounded by the viola. The texture becomes thicker in the course of the piece, due in the main to the euphonistic demi-semiquaver figuration that surrounds the main subject. Then, a dance-like presto section in modal tonality interrupts the gentle flow of the variations. Towards the end, the main idea of the first movement is quoted. The emotional climax of the work is formed by the third movement, a trans-cendental cradle song of unearthly melodic beauty and lyrical tenderness. 'Today I have written down my sweetest longings ... Today, I have succeeded in writing a piece in which the earth begins to tremble. This will be my best . . . Here, I can find a place for my most beautiful melodies'—thus Janáček describes this part of the quartet to Mme. Stoesslová. The movement begins in a modally inflected C flat major, rising climactically to an Adagio middle part whose love song seems to reveal all the tragic depth of his late passion. The opening theme of the Finale is a dancing whole-tone melody in Janáček's Russian manner. This sprightly subject is soon joined by a second idea, based on wide interval leaps which, propounded by the second violin, breaks out in a mighty *furioso* cadenza (bars 231–238). 'Now I must still succeed with the last movement. It shall reflect the anguish I feel about you', is what the composer wrote to his friend. He must have had the above mentioned passage in mind.

As with other late works of Janáček, the quartet is stylistically more rounded; the contrasts, plentiful as always, are more moderate; anything bizarre or grotesque is eschewed. The harmonic structure, if compared with works such as the *First String Quartet* or the *Concertino*, is simpler and predominantly diatonic; yet Janáček's late predilection for chords and melodies using the interval of the fourth is here, too, strongly in evidence. Modal and whole-tone elements are also frequent.

Janáček's piano style stems from the clear-cut formalism of classical tradition on the one hand, and from the romantic, miniaturistic mood-picture of the later nineteenth century on the other. Clearly conceived lines and thematic conciseness are allied to the poetic and expressive art of Schumann and the Russians, mainly Moussorgsky. On a classical-romantic basis stand his early piano compositions, such as the Schumannesque *Variations in G minor* which he composed when a student in Leipzig (1880) and dedicated to Zdenka Schulz. In this work—it is now obtainable in printed form—his striving for a virile style of expression and preference for short, contrasting sections are already evident.

In the cycle, *On an Overgrown Path* (*Na zarostlém chodníčku*, 1902-8) Janáček's piano style has gained full individual stature, notwithstanding the fact that five pieces of the first part—'Our Evenings' ('Naše večeřy'), 'A Blown-Away Leaf' ('Listek odvanutý'), 'The Virgin of Frýdek' ('Frýdecká Pana Maria'), 'Good Night' ('Dobrou noc'), 'The Little Owl Continues Screeching' ('Sýček neodletěl') and the last numbers of the second part were originally set for harmonium. In their sharply-limned expressive style, these miniatures preserve memories from the composer's youth. On this path, overgrown indeed by the passing of the years, the fifty-year-old composer wanders back to his native village. Images of long ago rise up: the yearning duet at eventide, 'Our evenings'; the timid melody of 'A blown-away leaf', dying away after a beginning of nine bars, followed by the whirlwind of the middle part; the teasing 'Come away with us' ('Podše s námi'), based on a verbal tag of the Lachian district; the tender vision of 'The Virgin of Frýdek', where a solemn procession seems to approach, surrounded by the strains of the organ; the gossiping children of the Hukvaldy school house in 'They chattered like swallows' ('Šebetaly jak vlastovičky'); the reticent Moussorgskian 'The word fails' ('Nelze domluvit'); 'Good night', a childlike, pious melody, mysteriously enlivened by a flickering semiquaver motive; the halting, anxious 'So utterly anxious' ('Tak neskonále úzko'); and lastly the uncanny nature sound of the hooting owl. The five numbers of the second part are published without title; but it is more than likely that here, too, Janáček had definite poetic situations in mind. The first piece in E flat major with its free metre and improvisatory character, and the subsequent one in G flat major, based on Janáček's favourite 'Intonation-motifs' (major third—major second), are rooted in folk music. The scherzoid third piece—this and No. 5 were added at a later date—is followed by a stormy E flat major movement (No. 4), and the rhetorical No. 5 that dies away in an Adagio. These miniatures are full of Janáček's uncanny intensity of experiencing life. Well-defined sentiment and acute observation help to make every piece a little drama in itself. The leading melody in most of the pieces lies in the treble, frequently set for one or two parts and usually accompanied by an ostinato-like middle part (cp. Ex. 42 a, b,); sometimes the whole texture is held together by a bass of sustained notes (cp. Ex. 42 c,).

Example 42

a) 'In the Mist' No. 1
b) 'Our Evenings'
c) 'The Virgin of Frýdek'

While the miniatures of the *Overgrown Path* depict a period of life in retrospect, transfigured by distance and intimacy of form, the *Sonata* 1.10.1905 wrestles with life in all its actuality—a spontaneous reaction to a tragic event, to which a topical political and national note is added. This sonata in two movements was inspired by the death of a Czech worker, František Pavlík, who had been killed when a street demonstration in favour of founding a Czech university at Brno was broken up by Austrian soldiers. The two movements in Janáček's most sombre E flat minor, entitled 'Premonition' and 'Death', are a heroic epitaph in sound. The piano style is full, in places rough, but all times passionately expressive. Above pianissimo broken chords, there spreads the first movement's sorrowful main melody, which subsequently is to gain shattering emotional pathos. At the fourth bar, it is suddenly severed by a sharp semiquaver ostinato—a figure breaking in like the grim reality of the fusillade on the demonstrators. The ostinato-figure remains united to the main subject, and in its shortened version it supplies the driving force of the middle part (development section). A lyrical second subject carries a certain relaxation and contrast into the tempestuous mood of the movement, which closes with a sonata-form recapitulation. The theme of the Adagio, given out in octaves, has grown from the ostinato motif of the first movement—an example of the very personal manner in which Janáček is able to transform a melodic idea, particularly in its intrinsic, poetical character. The brisk semiquaver-figure becomes here a plangent symbol of grief, and is subsequently transmuted into an inexorable, heroic theme of fate.

Example 43

    a) Sonata, 1st movement

    b) Sonata, 2nd movement

This sonata was originally planned in three movements—the third movement, however, was destroyed by Janáček, and it is only by a happy accident that the preceding pieces were preserved from a similar fate.

More reflective and of less spontaneous inspiration are the four piano pieces *In the Mist* (*V mlhách*, 1912). They, too, are miniatures, possibly with a hidden programme. The first has a questing theme of seconds, accompanied by an ostinato (cp. Ex. 43 a) and interrupted by impressionistic passages and chord-motifs. The next piece is an Adagio with a heavy, yearning, singable theme, broadly harmonised, relieved by gossamer demisemiquaver figures in pianissimo, and eventually worked up to an emotional outbreak. The third piece begins like a folk song, develops into a march-like middle part, and ebbs away with the initial melody. The cycle is brought to an end by a lively Finale—tempestuous, and again reflective, refreshing in its linear directness, though in places a little crude.

In his youth, Janáček composed a few organ works: a *Choral Fantasy* (it is not extant) which made a great impression at the

exams at the Prague organ school, and two Adagio movements—
Concerto Fantasias—which he published himself in 1884.
Max Brod had drawn attention to the interesting fact[1] that even
in these early works long before Janáček occupied himself with
the speech-motifs, his abrupt, melodically short-winded, rhythmically irregular style may be found. Brod drew from this the
conclusion that 'it may have been his inborn traits of energy,
stamina and decisiveness which led Janáček to the observation of
the equally sharply defined language of the people; in consequence, the figurations typical of his subsequent works may
pertain of extrinsic as well as intrinsic qualities.' It is a well-known
fact that certain pre-dispositions in the nature of an artist make
him particularly apt to absorb impressions and experiences which
prove to be specially congenial to his artistic personality and which
proceed to determine his individual style. In Janáček's case, this
phenomenon is further proof for the absolute genuineness of his
art and the deep, organic logic of his development.

Apart from the Intermezzo for organ in the *Glagolitic Mass*,
mentioned in another context, Janáček wrote no further
compositions for organ.

[1]Max Brod, Leoš Janáček, p. 31.

CATALOGUE OF WORKS

I. COMPOSITIONS FOR PIANO

Lost

Dumka (performed 8. 9. 1879)

Sonata I. (completed 6. 10. 1879, Leipzig)

Nokturno (16. 10. 1879, Leipzig)

Funeral March—Smuteční pochod (10. 12. 1879, Leipzig)

17 Fugues (9. 10. 1879—12. 1. 1880, Leipzig)

Zdenka's Minuet—Zdenčin menuet (8. 1. 1880, Leipzig)

Rondo (Jan. 1880)

Sonata II. (10.—14. 4. 1880, Vienna)

Transcription of the Song The Hazelbush—Oříšek léskový (5. 3. 1899)

Spring Song—Jarní píseň, cycle (1912)

In Memory—Na památku (Brno, no date)

Unfinished

To the Dog Čipera (8. 8. 1925—23. 4. 1928)

I Wait for You—Čekám Tě (5. 8. 1928)

Complete

Thema con variazioni (Zdenka's variations, 20. 1.—22. 2. 1880, Leipzig)

Ej, danaj (2. 4. 1892)

National Dances of Moravia—Národní tance na Moravě (Brno 1895, H.M. 1950)

On an Overgrown Path—Na zarostlém Chodníčku (1902–08, H.M. 1947)

Moravian Dances—Moravské tance (Čeladenský, Pilky, about 1904, A. Piša, Brno 1905)

Sonata 1. x. 1905 (A street Scene—Z ulice, H.M. 1924, 1949)

Reminiscence—Vzpomínka (8. 5. 1928, Muzika,
Belgrade 1928, Melpa 1936)

In the Mist—V mlhách (1912, H.M. 1929, 1938,
1944)

For Piano and Chamber Orchestra

Concertino (January—29. 4. 1925, H.M. 1926, 1949)

Capriccio for one hand (April—30. 10. 1926,
SNKLHU 1953)

March of the Bluetits—Pochod Modráčků
(19. 5. 1924; third movement of the wind
sextet Youth—Mládí, Hudební besídka, vol.
IV, 1927/8)

II. COMPOSITIONS FOR ORGAN

Planned and unfinished
Sonata (1895/6)

Lost

Choral Fantasy—Fantasie choralní (performed
23. 7. 1875)

Unfinished

Composition for Organ (4. 8. 1878, Oettingen,
opening of the fuge, publ. Helfert, Janáček,
supplement, p. 9)

Complete

Compositions for Organ (two Concerto Fantasias—
Adagio—1880, Brno, 1884)

II. CHAMBER MUSIC

For Violin

Lost

Sonnet for Solo Violin and String Orchestra—
Znělky pro sólové housle s průvodem smyč.

orchestru (about 1876, performed about 1876/7)

Seven Romances (26. 10.–16. 11. 1879, Leipzig, No. 4 only preserved)

Sonata I. (14. 1. 1880–18. 1. 1880, Leipzig)

Sonata II. (20. 4.–12. 5. 1880, Vienna)

Unfinished

Violin Concerto 'Pilgrimage of the Soul'— Putování dušičky (1927–28, partly used in the overture of the opera The House of the Dead)

The Gnat—Komár (sketch, sul ponticello)

Complete

Romance No. 4 (finished 16. 11. 1879, Leipzig, H.M. 1938, 1949)

Dumka (1880, H.M. 1929, 1945, also in Ten pieces for violin and piano, No. 4, H.M. 1947)

Sonata III. (about 1913, revised 1913–1921, H.M. 1922, 1929, 1947)

Ballad for Violin and Piano (probably before 1913, publ. 1915)

For Cello

Fairy Tale—Pohádka (1st version finished 10. 2. 1910, 2nd version about 1923, H.M. 1924, 1949)

Presto (about 1910)

For Flute

Unfinished

Sanssouci for Flute and Piano or Harp (Lidové Noviny, Brno, 15. 5. 1924)

For Clarinet

Lost

Minuet and Scherzo (about 1880)

For Chamber Music Ensemble

> *Lost*
>
>> Sarabande for String Quintet (perf. 8. 12. 1878)
>> Piano Trio (Autumn 1908, revised 1909)
>> String Quartet O. (25. 5–June 1880, Vienna)
>
> *Complete*
>
>> String Quartet I. after Tolstoy's Kreutzersonata First String Quartet, 30. 10. 1923–7. 11. 1923, based on the Piano Trio, H.M. 1925, 1945, parts H.M. 1948)
>>
>> String Quartet II. (Second String Quartet, Intimate Letters—Listy důvěrné, between 29. 1.– 19. 2. 1928, H.M. 1938, 1949)
>>
>> Youth—Mládí, Suite for Wind Sextet (1924, H.M. 1925, 1947)

IV. ORCHESTRAL MUSIC

> *Lost*
>
>> Scherzo to a Symphony (25. 1. 1880, Leipzig)
>> Funeral March (finished 10. 12. 1879, Leipzig, perf. 20. 3. 1898 as a movement from the oratorio Amarus)
>> Moderato (about 1904)
>
> *Complete*
>
>> Suite for String Orchestra (about 1877, perf. 2. 12. 1877, O. Pazdírek, Brno, 1926, Orbis Prague, 1926)
>>
>> Idyll—Idylla for String Orch. (31. 7.–24. 8. 1878, Orbis 1951)
>>
>> Valachian Dances (1889–90, Bursík & Kohout, Prague 1890, as Lachian Dances H.M. 1928, 1948, Orbis 1951)
>>
>> Hanakian Dances (10 dances for piano for 2 and 4

hands, also for orch. or chorus and orch, about 1889/90, some used in the ballet Rákocz, Rákoczy, publ. Folkdances from Moravia)

Suite for Full Orchestra op. 3, also known as Serenade (finished Jan. 1891, U.E., Vienna, 1930)

Adagio for Full Orchestra (about 1891)

Quadrille for Symphonic Orchestra (identical with the music of the piano piece The Turning Spinningwheel)

Kozáček, Russian nat. dance for orch. (finished 9. 12. 1899)

Serbian Kolo for Orch. Nat. Dance (about 1899)

Jealousy—Žárlivost (Overture to Jenufa for full orch. finished 31. 12. 1894)

The Fiddler's Child—Šumařovo dítě, ballad for full orch. (1912, perf. Prague 14. 11. 1917, H.M. 1924, 1949)

Taras Bulba, Rhapsody for Full Orch. (1915–29. 3. 1918, perf. Brno 9. 10. 1921, piano score H.M. 1925, orch. score H.M. 1927, 1947)

Ballad of the Blaník—Ballada Blanická, symph. poem for full orch. (finished 1920, perf. Brno 21. 3. 1920)

Sinfonietta, also Military Sinfonietta for Full Orch. (finished 1. 4. 1926, perf. Prague 29. 6. 1926, orch. score Philharmonia, Vienna and U.E. Vienna)

Danube—Dunaj, symph. poem in four parts (1923–28, finished by O. Chlubna, perf. Brno 2. 5. 1948)

V. SONGS

Planned but not carried out
Song of a Slave

Lost

Die Abendschoppen, song (25. 10. 1879, Leipzig)

Song (10. 11. 1879, Leipzig)

Fruehlingsbilder, cycle of songs (23. 4.–7. 5. 1880, Vienna)

Songs with the accomp. of the piano (perf. Brno, 5. 3. 1899)

Complete

Song of Spring—Jarní píseň (1879, revised 1905, O. Pazdírek, Brno, 1944)

Diary of a Young Man who Vanished—Zápisník zmizelého, for tenor, alto and 3 female voices with piano (Sept. 1917–6. 6. 1919, perf. Brno 18. 4. 1921; O. Pazdíred, Brno 1921, SNKLHU 1953)

Nursery Rhymes—Říkadla for 9 voices, piano, and 11 instruments (1925, revised 1927, perf. 25. 4. 1927; U.E. Vienna 1928)

ARRANGEMENTS OF FOLK SONGS

Královničky (10 numbers, about 1889, perf. Brno 21. 2. 1889, SNKLHU 1954)

Bouquet of Moravian Folk Songs (Kytice s národ. písní moravských, about 1890, E. Scholz, Telč 1890, 1892, 1901, H.M. 1929, 1947)

Folk Poetry of Hukvaldy in Songs—Ukvalská lidová poesie v písních (1898, A. Píša, Brno 1899, H.M. 1929, 1949)

Folk Songs of Hukvaldy—Ukvalské písně, 6 folksongs (1899, H.M. 1949)

Let's go, dearest, let's go—Podme, milá, podme
(1911)

Kreuzpolka—Krajcpolka (about 1912)

26 Popular Ballads—26 balad lidových:

  6 folksongs (10. 12. 1909, H.M. 1922)

  Folk Nokturnes-Lidová Nokturna (1906, H.M.
    1922, 1950)

  Folk Songs of Detvany—Písně detvanské
    (1916)

  Ballads of Zbojnice—Zbojnické balady (1916,
    H.M. 1950)

  Five Folk Songs for Male Choir and Piano—5
    nár. písní (1916/17).

Songs of Silesia—Slezské písně (1918, Svoboda,
  Brno, 1920, 4 numbers arranged by B. Bakala
  with the accomp. of flute, violin, viola and
  cello, 1951)

Folk Songs of Moravia—Moravské lidové písně
  (1922, H.M. 1950)

Folk Songs for Voice and Piano—Lidové písně
  pro zpěv a klavír

Ballad—Balada, folksong and piano,

Ej, duby, duby

I have a Family—Rodinu mám

EDITION OF FOLK SONGS

  Folk Songs of Moravia, newly collected—Národní
    písně moravské v nově nasbírané (1897, Czech
    akademy, Prague 1901)

  Love Songs of Moravia—Moravské písně milostné
    (1924, Nat. Instit. for Folksongs, Prague 1930–
    36)

VI. CHORUSES

Male choirs

Lost

Ženich v nucený (about 1873, perf. 27. 4. 1873)

Complete

Ploughing—Orání (1873, H.M. 1923, 1929, 1948)

War Song—Válečná, with piano accomp., trump. and 3 tromb. (1873, H.M.)

Inconsistency in Love—Nestálost lásky (1873)

Forsaken—Osamělá bez těchy (1874, rev. 1898, 1925)

True Love—Láska opravdivá (1976, Melpa 1937)

If you don't love me, what do I care—Když mne nechceš, což je vícs (1875/6, perf. Brno 23. 1. 1876)

Elegy—Zpěvná duma (1876)

How Strange my Lover is—Divím se milému (about 1875/6, Melpa 1937)

You will not Escape Fate—Osudu neujdeš (1878)

Two Pigeons are Sitting on a Fir Tree—Na košatej jedly dva holubi šeďá (about 1880)

At the Ferry—Na prievoze (about 1883–85)

Four Male Choruses—Mužské sbory:

Warning—Výhrůžka

Oh, Love—O, lásko

War, War,—Ach, vojna

Your Lovely Eyes—Krásné oči Tvé (about June 1885, K. Winkler, Brno, 1886, later publ. H.M. 1924, 1948, under the title Čtveřice mužských sborů, dedicated to Ant. Dvořák)

Jealousy—Žárlivec (14. 5. 1888)

Our Birch Tree—Což ta naše bříza (18. 4. 1893,
H.M. 1929, 1949)

Little Wreath—Vínek (1893, H.M. 1929, 1948)

The Sun has Risen—Už je slunko z tej hory ven
(1893)

Festival Chorus—Slavnostní sbor (1897)

Four Moravian Choruses for Male Voices—Čtvero
mužských sborů moravských:

Now you Know—Dež víš

The Gnats—Komáři

The Witch—Klekánica

Farewell—Rozloučení (1904, M. Urbánek,
Prague 1906, H.M. 1950, Nr. 1 and 3 in
German, Leipzig 1908)

Kantor Halfar (about 24. 10. 1906, H.M. 1923,
1948)

Maryčka Magdonová (1st version autumn 1906,
2nd version spring 1907, F. Urbánek, Prague
1909, H.M. 1950)

Seventy-thousand—Sedmdesát tisíc (Dec. 1909,
F. Urbánek, Prague 1912, H.M. 1923, 1929)

The Featherbed—Peřina (about 1914, H.M. 1929,
1948)

The Czech Legion—Česká legie (18. 11. 1918)

The Foolish Tramp—Potulný šílenec (1. 11. 1922,
H.M. 1925)

Our Flag—Naše vlajka (1925–1926)

Chorus composed for the occasion of the laying of
the foundation stone of the Masaryk University, Brno (2. 4. 1928)

Female choirs

Songs of Hradčany—Hradčanské písničky (1916,
H.M. 1922)

The Wolf's Trace—Vlčí stopa (25. 1. 1916)

Kašpar Rucký (12. 11. 1916, H.M. 1925, 1938)

Mixed choirs

Lost

Folk Song of Serbia—Srbská lidová píseň (perf. 27. 4. 1873)

Complete

Festival Chorus—Slavnostní sbor (1877)

Autumn Song—Písen v jeseni (18. 9. 1880, Orbis 1950)

The Wild Duck—Kačena divoká (about 1885, Orbis 1950)

Our Song—Naše píseň (1890, Orbis 1950)

Elegy at the death of Janáček's daughter, Olga, Russian text by M. N. Vevercová, 28. 4. 1903, rev. 28. 3. 1904)

When we Went to the Fair—Keďjsme šli na hody

The Gnats' Wedding—Komáři se ženili

I Planted the Greens (three choruses with orch. from the ballet Rákocz Rákoczy, no dates, unpubl.)

Moravian Duets—Moravské dvojzpěvy (arrangements of 6 duets by Ant. Dvořák, 1877 and 1884, private print by J. Plavec, Prague 1939)

VII. CANTATAS

Planned but not carried out

Song of Peace—Píseň míru (about 1928)

Complete

Amarus (about 1898, rev. 1901 and 1906, perf. 2. 12. 1900, vocal score and parts H.M. 1938)

Na Soláni Čarták (1911, perf. 20. 3. 1912)

The Everlasting Gospel—Věčné evangelium (1914, perf. 5. 2. 1917)

Glagolitic Mass (2. 8.–15. 10. 1926, perf. Brno
5. 12. 1927, vocal score U. E. Vienna, 1928)
Olaf Trygvason (piano arrangement of the cantata
by Ed. Grieg, about 1902)

CHURCH MUSIC

Lost

Mass (composed during the eighteen-seventies)
Sanctus (18–23. 11. 1879, Leipzig)

Complete

Graduale in festo purificationis B. V. Mariae (about
1870, revised 28. 1. 1887)
Take your Rest—Odpočiň si (about 1875, H.M.
1926)
Exaudi Deus (Cecilie IV, 1877)
Regnum Mundi (about 1878)
Ten Czech religious songs from Lehner's canzionale
(1881, publ. K. Winkler, Brno, 1881/2, 2nd
edition 1889)
O Lord—Hospodiňe (1896, perf. Brno 19. 4. 1896)
Veni sancte spiritus (about 1900)
Our Father—Otče náš; also: Moravský Otče náš
(1901)
Sanct Wenceslas—Svatý Václave (organ accomp.
about 1902)
Constitues (before 1903, rev. 15. 7. 1903)
Ave Maria (January 1904, soprano, violin and
organ)
Hail Mary—Zdrávas Maria (chorus, tenor solo and
organ, no date)
Czech religious polyphonic songs from the Příbor
cancionale—Církevní zpěvy české vícehlasné

z Příborského kancionálu (about 1904, 4 numbers)

Mass after Liszt's *Messe pour orgue* (arranged 24. 9. 1901)

The Lord Christ is Born—Narodil se Christus Pan (arrangement Hud. besídka 1926/7)

Lullaby—Ukolébavka (piano accmp. to J. A. Komenský's Lullaby, Hud, besídka, 1927/8)

Unfinished

Mass in E flat major (1907/8, completed by V. Petrželka, perf. 7. 3. 1943, Brno)

VIII. OPERAS

Planned but not carried out

Athalia (1884, after Racine)

The Miser (1884, after Molière)

Song of Spring—Jarní píseň (about April 1904, after G. Preissová)

The Bells' Soul—Duše zvonů (1906, after Q. M. Vyskočil)

Maryša (July 1908, after the brothers Mrštík)

Ondráš (about 1916–20, after A. Chamrád)

The Child—Dítě (10. 7. 1923, after F. X. Šalda)

Unfinished or sketchy

Angels Sonata—Andělská Sonata (June 1903, after J. Merhaut)

Gazdina Roba (April 1904 and Aug. 1907, after G. Preissová)

The Adventures of the Last of the Abencerage—Příhody posledního Abencerage (1885/6, after R. Chateaubriand)

John the Hero—Honza hrdina (29. 6. 1905, after K. Dostál-Tutinov)

The Mintmaster's Wife—Paní mincmistrová (1906/
7, after L. Stroupežnický)

Anna Karenina (from 5–29. 1. 1907, after L. N.
Tolstoy)

The Living Corpse—Živá mrtvola (September
1916, after L. N. Tolstoy)

Divoška (October 1920, after V. Krylov)

Schluck und Jau (incidental music to the play by
Gerhart Hauptmann, May 1928, Introduction
and 3 numbers)

Complete

Šárka—Opera in 3 acts (Jul. Zeyer, first version
January–August 1887, second version finished
June 1888, third version before August 1918,
final revision probably 1924, perf. Brno
11. 11. 1925)

Beginning of a Romance—Počátek románu, One
act (Libretto Gabr. Preissová and Jar. Tichý,
15. 5.–2. 9. 1891, perf. Brno 10. 2. 1894,
unpublished)

Jenufa—Její pastorkyňa, Moravian musical drama
in 3 acts (Libretto Gabr. Preissová, 18. 3. 1894–
18. 3. 1903, revised 1906, 1911, 1916, perf.
Brno 21. 1. 1904, Prague 26. 5. 1916, vocal
score Klub přátel umění v Brně 1908, H.M.
1917, 1934, 1943, 1949; orch. score and vocal
score with German text by Max Brod, U.E.
Vienna 1917)

Destiny—Osud, opera in 3 scenes (Libretto Leoš
Janáček and Fedora Bartošová, Nov. 1903–
May 1904, broadcast performance Brno,
18. 9. 1934, in manuscript, stage perf. Brno,
1958)

The Excursions of Mr. Brouček—Výlety pana Broučka (Part I. Excursion of Mr. Brouček to the Moon, Libretto Svatopluk Čech, adapted by V. Dyk, K. Mašek, Z. Janke, F. Gellner, J. Mahen and F. S. Procházka, 1908–1917; Part II. Excursion of Mr. Brouček to the XVth century, Libretto Svatopluk Čech, adapted by F. S. Procházka, 1917; both parts perf. Prague 23. 4. 1920, vocal score U.E. Vienna 1919)

Kátà Kabanová, opera in 3 acts (after the play The Storm by A. N. Ostrovsky, translated by V. Červinka, Nov. 1919–17. 2. 1921, perf. Brno 23. 11. 1921, vocal score U.E. Vienna 1924)

The Cunning Little Vixen—Příhody lišky Bystroušky, opera in 3 acts (after Rud. Těsnohlídek, 1921–March 1923, perf. Brno 6. 11. 1924, vocal score U.E. Vienna 1924)

The Makropulos case—Věc Makropulos, opera in 3 acts (Karel Čapek, 11. 11. 1923–12. 11. 1925, perf. Brno 18. 12. 1926, vocal score U.E. Vienna 1926)

The House of the Dead—Z mrtvého domu, opera in 3 acts (after F. M. Dostoievsky, Febr. 1927–8. 6. 1928, perf. Brno 12. 4. 1930, vocal score also with German Text by Max Brod, U.E. Vienna 1930)

IX. BALLETS

Planned but not carried out

Below the Radhošt—Pod Radhoštem (1888/9)

Unfinished

> Valachian Dances—Valšské tánce, An idyll in 1 act
> (scenarium with 11 dance scenes, about 1890)

Complete

> Rákocz Rákoczy (Libretto Jan Herben, May 1891,
> perf. Prague 24. 7. 1891, revised by Rud.
> Walter and perf. Brno 14. 5. 1938, Manuscript)

ABBREVIATIONS

HM=Hudební˙ Matice

SNKLHU=Statní nakladatelství krásné literatury, hudby a umění

U.E.=Universal Edition

BIBLIOGRAPHY

Max Brod: Leoš Janáček (Univ. Edition, Vienna, 1956)
Max Brod: Sternenhimmel (Kurt Wolff Verlag, Muenchen, 1933) Various essays on Janáček
Winton Dean: Janáček and Kátà Kabanová, The Listener, London, 1954
L. Firkušný: L. Janáček and the Brno theatre (Janáček a brňenské divadlo)
Vladimír Helfert: Leoš Janáček (O. Pazdírek, Brno, 1939)
Vladimír Helfert—Erich Steinhard: Music in Czechoslovakia (Die Musik in der tschecho-slovakischen Republik (Orbis, Praha, 1938)
Hans Hollander: Leoš Janáček and his Operas (The Musical Quarterly, New York, 1928)
Hans Hollander: The Music of Leoš Janáček—its origin in folklore (The Musical Quarterly New York, 1955)
Hans Hollander: Leoš Janáček—Slav Genius (Music and Letters, London, 1941)
Hans Hollander : Leoš Janáček—A Centenary Appreciation (The Musical Times, London, 1954)
Hans Hollander : Leoš Janáček—Zum hundertsten Geburtstag (Schweizerische Musik-zeitung, Zuerich)
Hans Hollander: Leoš Janáček und seine Orchesterwerke (Schweizerische Musikzeitung, Zuerich, 1956)
Hans Hollander: Janáček's Last Opera (The Musical Times, London, 1956)
Hans Hollander: Erinnerungen an Leoš Janáček (Blaetter der Staatsoper, Berlin, 1931)
Hans Hollander: Leoš Janáček und sein 'Tagebuch eines Verschollenen' (Radio Wien, 1932)
Leoš Janáček: Tonality in folk song (O toniňe v lidové písni (Narodopisný věstník českoslovanský, XVIII, 1926)
Leoš Janáček: Structure and connexion of chords (O skladbé souzvukuv a jejích spojuv (F. A. Urbánek, Praha, 1897)
Leoš Janáček: Folk song and Folk music (O lidove pisni a lidove hudbe) (Statní nakla-datelství krásné literatury a umění, Praha 1955)
Leoš Janáček: Interview in Die literarische Welt, 1927
Leoš Janáček: Complete treatise of Harmony (Uplná nauka o harmonii) (F. Piša, Brno, 1920)
Leoš Janáček: Speech melodies in our language (Nápěvky naše mluvy) (Časopis mora-vského musea, 1903)
Leoš Janáček: Speech melodies in children's language (Nápěvky dětskě mluvy) (Český lid, 1902 and 1904)
Leoš Janáček: Essays from the Lidové Noviny (Edited Jan Racek and Leoš Firkušný, Brno, 1938)
Hynek Kašlík: L. Janáček as a Conductor (Leoš Janáček dirigent) (Knihovna unie čsl. hudenbníků z povolání, 1936)
Hynek Kašlík: K. Kovářovič's alterations in Janáček's opera Jenufa (Retuše Karla Ková-řoviče v Janáčkově opeře Její Pastorkyne) (Hudební vestník, Praha, 1939)
Correspondence of L. Janáček and F. S. Procházka (Hudební matice, Praha, 1949)
Correspondence of L. Janáček and Maria Calma and Dr. F. Veselý (Orbis, Praha, 1951)
Correspondence of Leoš Janáček and Max Brod (Statní nakladatelství krásné literatury, hudby a umění, Praha 1953)
Jaroslav Křička: Leoš Janáček's 'Eternal Gospel' (Leoše Janáčka 'Věcně evangelium'), (Hudební revue, 1917)
Colin Mason: Janáček a victim of history (The Listener, London, 1953)
Jan Mikota: Janáček in England (Janáček v Anglii) (Listy hudební matice, 1926)
Daniel Muller: Leoš Janáček (Edition Rieder, Paris, 1930)
Musikologie vol. 3 Various essays on Janáček's music (Statní nakladatelství krásné litera-tury, hudby a umění, Praha, 1955)
Rosa Newmarch: The music of Czechoslovakia (Oxford University Press, 1942)
Rosa Newmarch: Leoš Janáček and Moravian Music (The Slavonic Revue, 1922)

Jan Racek: Janáček's creative profile (Leoš Janáček, Poznámky k tvurčimu profilu, Index, Olomouc, 1938)—Essays on Janáček and the Music Drama; Janáček's relationship to the culture and music of Russia; Janáček's relationship to Smetana; Janáček and Prague; Janáček and the decorative arts; etc.

Jan Racek: The Slavonic foundations in the work of Leoš Janáček (Slovanské prvky v tvorbě Leoše Janáčka) (Brno, 1952)

Bohumír Stědron: Leoš Janáček at the Teachers' Training College in Brno (Leoš Janáček na mužském učitelském ústavu v Brné) (Tempo, XIII)

Bohumír Stědron: Leoš Janáček, Letters and Reminiscences (Artia, Praha, 1955)

Vladimír Úlehla: Živá písen (The Living Song) (Fr. Borovy, Praha, 1949)

Adolf E. Vašek: In the traces of Leoš Janáček (Po stopách Leoše Janáčka) (Brňenskě knižní nakladatelství, Brno, 1930)

Jaroslav Vogel: Janáček the dramatic artist (Janáček dramatik)

Jiří Vysloužil: Janáček's musico-folkloristic oeuvre (Hudebné folkloristické dílo Leoše Janáčka) (from L. Janáček; O lidové písni an lidové hudbě 1955)

Karel Vetterl: Folk Songs and Dances from Valašsko Kloboucka (Lidové písně a Dance a Valašsko Kloboucka) (Czechoslovak Academy of Sciences, Praha, 1955).

INDEX

NOTE: Numbers refer to pages; numbers in parentheses, printed next to a page number, refer to footnotes on that page.